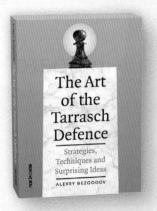

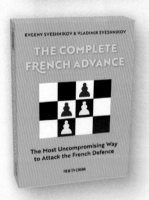

REYKJAVÍK OPEN 2018 ♞ BOBBY FISCHER MEMORIAL

KING OF CHESS

At this year's Reykjavík Open we celebrate the genius of Bobby Fischer. Ever since Fischer became the world champion of chess, in Reykjavík in 1972, we Icelanders have been prone to call him the King of Chess. Fischer´s contributions to chess history will be celebrated during the tournament. A special event will be organized on the "free day" on March 9th. A Fischer Random championship which will also be the European Fischer Random Cup in co-operation with the European Chess Union.

THE LEGACY OF FISCHER

Other tournament events will be dedicated to Fischer's chess life in many different ways. There will be lectures, exhibitions and you will get the opportunity to visit the playing hall from 1972, visit his final resting place, his favourite restaurant and of course see the original chess board at which he beat Boris Spassky, which now sits in the Icelandic National Museum.

A UNIQUE EVENT

The Reykjavík Open has been a unique event in Reykjavík since 1964 when Mikhael Tal was crowned king of chess in Reykjavík. The tournament has featured many of the strongest chess players in the world, along with Tal; Nona Gaprindashvili, David Bronstein, Vasili Smyslov, Bent Larsen, Friðrik Ólafsson, Nigel Short, Hikaru Nakamura, Hou Yifan, Fabiano Caruana, Judit Polgar, Wesley So, Levon Aronian and Magnus Carlsen.

A UNIQUE VENUE

The event will take place in Harpa music and conference Hall in downtown Reykjavík, by the Reykjavík harbour.

REYKJAVÍK OPEN

official sponsor GAMMA

'If you stumble, make it part of the dance.'

CONTRIBUTORS TO THIS ISSUE
Vishy Anand, Vladimir Barsky, Adhiban Baskaran, Jeroen Bosch, Fabiano Caruana, Maxim Dlugy, Daniil Dubov, John Henderson, David Howell, Larry Kaufman, Dylan McClain, Parimarjan Negi, Ian Nepomniachtchi, Peter Heine Nielsen, Maxim Notkin, Arthur van de Oude-weetering, Judit Polgar, Matthew Sadler, Nigel Short, Peter Svidler, Jan Timman

Monkey Business

It was the anonymous street artist Banksy, armed only with a rat stencil, cans of spray paint, a roller and some crafty nocturnal subterfuge, who literally overnight turned graffiti into an acceptable and very profitable part of the art establishment. Nowadays, with the growth in street art, every major city has opened up their walls and buildings to showcase emerging new talents.

A new addition to London's popular Urban Street Art Tours was seen in the early autumn after Graffiti artist 'Trafik' transformed a large building wall along Pedley Street, just off Brick Lane, close to the Old Spitalfields Market, with his formidable scene depicting a chimpanzee deliberating over a game of chess.

Trafik painted the three-story wall on a ladder purely with a mini-roller and some black and white paint for his striking visual effect. And if you think the simian chess image looks familiar, then that's because the artist based his work on a very famous 1954 *Daily Mirror* newspaper photo from their 'The Champion Chimps series' that can now be found in Getty Images: 'Pepe', the chess champion of Chimp Town.

© OLIVIER SUON, FLICKR

Oxford Blues

What do eight heads of state, including US president Bill Clinton, three Australian prime ministers, four Nobel laureates and the current woman's world No.1 chess player all have in common? The answer is that they were all awarded

Will Hou Yifan continue to play chess while studying in Oxford?

prestigious Rhodes scholarships to study as overseas students at Oxford. In mid-December, following a final of tough interviews in Shanghai, 23-year-old Hou Yifan became one of four Chinese students awarded Rhodes scholarships. She will take up her place this autumn, as she heads to the 'city of the dreaming spires', as famously coined by Victorian poet Matthew Arnold. Hou will study for an MSc in education. There were 12,000 applicants worldwide.

But will she continue to play chess while studying at Oxford? When she was asked the question at the start of the Tata Steel Tournament, Hou confidently replied: 'I hope to be able to play as much as possible.' So it looks as if she's set to take her place in the much-vaunted annual Varsity Chess Match between Oxford and Cambridge, the oldest continuous fixture on the chess calendar, with the rivalry over the 64 squares between these two fabled universities dating back to 1873.

Fortunes have waxed and waned over the years, but recently Cambridge has been in the ascendancy, and leads the historic series 59-54 (with 22 draws). While Hou won't become the first woman to play on Board 1 in the Varsity match – that particular glass ceiling was doubly smashed in 2000, when both top boards were defended by women: WGM Ruth Sheldon and IM Harriet Hunt – her appearance will tip the balance back in Oxford's favour, and she'll also become the first world No.1 (and ex-world champion, for that matter!) to play in the contest.

Drink like a Grandmaster

It looks like the fabled Moscow Central Chess Club is set for a little healthy competition with a swish new club opening its doors in the Russian capital. And while the Central Chess Club is dedicated to the honour of Mikhail Botvinnik, this one could well be a fitting tribute to Mikhail Tal, because it is claiming to be the only chess club with a bar!

Launched in one of Moscow's Stalin-era skyscrapers on Kudrinskaya Square, 'World Chess Club Moscow' – backed by Ilya Merenzon of Agon/World Chess – is marketing itself as a place where a new generation of chess enthusiasts can come to play while socializing over cocktails served by chief bartender Kenan Assab – hailed as one of the top bartenders in Moscow, according to Russian Esquire magazine.

On its Facebook page, the venue

The well-stocked bar at the new World Chess Club Moscow.

describes itself as the 'only chess club in the world with a bar'. Inside, the phrase 'I love you and chess' glows in neon lighting on the wall and there are chess sets around the bar, with the cocktails we mentioned earlier all named after world champions. Not only that, but they also offer private booths where chess lessons can be arranged with grandmasters.

And it is said that the investors behind the venture are looking to expand into other cities, including London, Berlin and New York.

Long live the King!

Fake news being circulated in America? Surely not! Pride of place outside the World Chess Hall of Fame in St. Louis, there stands a giant wooden king that we've always been led to

The Belgian king that tops the 'World's Largest Chess Piece' in St. Louis.

believe from the media to be the 'World's Largest Chess Piece', measuring in at 14.5 feet and weighing 2,280 pounds. It says so in the Guinness Book of Records, so it has to be true, right?

Well, wrong it seems – and by over two feet! It turns out that the St. Louis king is not the largest chess piece in the world after all, as that record was 'claimed' in 2014 with a European wooden king which measures in at a whopping 16 feet 7 inches tall and 6 feet 8 inches diameter at its base. It was presented and measured in

Kalmthout, Belgium, on 4 April 2014... by, er, those ever-reliable people at Guinness World Records!

It was all enough for Rex Sinquefield to call in to his own Saint Louis Chess Club live broadcast during the London Chess Classic, as he officially confirmed the shock news to a stunned Yasser Seirawan. But never fear, because the mega-rich chess patron – who never knew a problem that couldn't be solved by throwing money at it – promises to 'fix this anomaly very soon', to once again re-establish his home town's reputation in the giant chess piece arms race.

Last words

Who needs the 'Sofia Rules' to banish draws when we have the example of redoubtable characters in the game such as 'proud Yorkshireman' John Toothill? Sadly the ex-spy died aged 79 in late November after falling ill while playing in a league match at his local Windermere Chess Club. But he left us with an indefatigable fighting spirit right to the very end.

Reading his very colourful obituary in *The Westmoreland Gazette*, we discovered that the former Oxford student was a Russian linguist stationed in West Berlin during the Cold War, where he worked for the RAF to spy on Russian aircraft; a keen hillwalker who then took up the dream role of National Park Officer for the Lake District, and was

John Toothill: 'Draw? No way!'

awarded an OBE by the Queen on his retirement for his services to the environment. He was also a strong correspondence player, and part of the gold winning Great Britain team at the 1982 Correspondence Chess Olympiad, and the British Senior Champion in 2000.

As we say, he was playing chess when he was struck down in the middle of a game – but what really endeared him to our hearts was reading the following comment in the newspaper from his daughter, Dr Jane Toothill: 'The guy he was playing chess with offered him a draw in the ambulance – but he was doing well and he said no.'

Bite the Bullet

As everyone celebrated the arrival of 2018, for Magnus Carlsen and Hikaru Nakamura the old year hung around a little bit longer as they duked it out in the 2017 Chess.com Speed Chess Championship Final (sponsored by Garry Kasparov's MasterClass). Due to a busy schedule for both players, the final had to be extended into the new year and was played on 3 January.

It was a repeat of the 2016 final, which Carlsen had won relatively comfortably, beating Nakamura 14½-10½ to take the inaugural title – but just four days after winning the World Blitz crown in Riyadh, Carlsen was still on fire as he romped to an emphatic 18-9 match victory, dominating Nakamura from start to finish by winning all three blitz time controls, and even beating the American speed maven for the first time in a bullet contest.

The big winning margin mattered as the prize-money split was determined by the final score, with Carlsen taking $8,333.33 and Nakamura $1,666.67. The total amount Carlsen earned overall in the knockout tournament was $17,525.11 with $10,493.25 going to Nakamura.

The only conciliation for Nakamura

was that, as expected, he 'won' the Chess960 mini-match, 2½-½. This will at least give the unofficial 'Chess960 World Champion' some bragging rights with another battle with Carlsen on the horizon, a Chess960 Exhibition Match in February at the Hening Onstad Art Centre in Bærum, Norway. Nakamura will be disappointed that he

Magnus Carlsen won all three blitz controls against Hikaru Nakamura but lost 2½-½ in the Chess960 mini-match.

squandered several good winning positions that would have made the match much tighter. Carlsen by comparison was ruthless in converting any winning chances, such as this little gem from the bullet session.

Carlsen-Nakamura
chess.com speed 1'+1" 2017-18
position after 21...♖a3

22.b6! A very clever tactic that comes like a thunderbolt in Bullet. **22...c6** The point is that 22...cxb6 23.♘b5 wins material. Also no use is 22...♖xc3 23.♖e4! ♕c5 24.♗xc3 ♕xc3 25.♖c4 followed by 26.♖xc7, winning. **23.♘e4 ♘f5 24.♗b4 ♖a2 25.♗c5 ♕d7 26.♖a1 ♖xc2 27.♖a7 ♕d5 28.♖b1 ♖xc5 29.b7 g5 30.b8♕** Black resigned. ∎

Formats and time controls (2)

Thanks for the latest excellent issue, New In Chess 2017/8. As I read that you would like to hear from other readers what they think about Denny Helmuth's request to provide more detailed information about the time controls of published games (see p. 13), I have to say that I am missing this information, too. Some decisions or even blunders are more understandable if they were taken or committed in a blitz or rapid game.

Reinhard Pitz
Aix-la-Chapelle, Germany

Formats and time controls (3)

As a follow-up to the letter of Denny Helmuth in New In Chess 2017/8, I agree 100%. Knowing the tournament format (that is, Open, invitational, etc.) and the time controls is critical, I believe, for both understanding and appreciating the play of the tournament participants.

I have all issues of New In Chess since its inception and have noticed an increasing propensity of top-level players to either invoke main line openings to the nth degree beyond move 20 etc. or radically diverge in the opening with previously questionable variations. I'm sure such choices are in large part determined by the format of the chess event.

Secondly, over the last few years, your magazine has increasingly resorted to publishing games without opening moves, but starting at some middlegame position. Is it too much trouble to provide the opening moves from the start? GM Polgar's column invariably provides games positions but rarely complete game scores. Why should I look at a position without knowing from which opening it is derived? There is a limit to retrograde analysis even for us patzers!

Finally, My favourite column for many years now is IM Bosch's SOS. I don't always agree with his analysis but he has provided great food for thought. I have adopted two or three of his ideas and mostly with success.

Michael Allard
Bowie, MD, USA

Editorial postscript:

Thank you for your thoughts. We will always try to indicate what kind of time controls were used, although we understand that for some readers this information could be even more detailed. As for positions that are published without the opening moves, this we only do when it is this position that the author wants to say something about and when the preceding moves or the opening are not that relevant.

The physical side

I wish to challenge the lazy preconceptions held by Roy Keane and Jennifer Vallens in New In Chess 2017/8. We may not break our opponents' legs, or end up in the Betty Ford Clinic, but there is a physical side to chess, and one that is more serious than Roy or Jennifer imagine. The list of prominent chess players who have suffered heart disease at the peak of their careers is long. Attitudes and lifestyles are changing, but recent research indicates that stress does not just contribute to risk levels, but is a risk factor in itself for heart disease. Perhaps the news for chess is not so good.

Michael Kwan
Munich, Germany

Sad little thing

I was so inspired by Ding Liren's brilliant game published in New In Chess 2017/8. I especially enjoyed his humble notes (one can imagine how Alekhine would have embellished all that he 'saw'). It brought back those feelings of awe from my

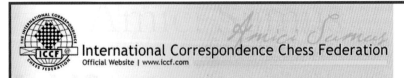

childhood whilst pondering the games of Morphy and Anderssen (and now AlphaZero?). Liren's pieces truly danced and seemed to engage me in dialogue as I followed their steps. But as scintillating as the tactics were, what struck me most was the lone figure in Black's army that failed to show up for work. The hapless a-pawn. I found myself loathing it, casting blame for its apparent apathy in time of crisis! I was reminded of a similar situation – a reverse situation actually – one of my favourite chess authors, Jan Hein Donner, wrote about in his essay titled 'Sweet Little Thing' (*The King: Chess Pieces*, pp.112-117), where he detailed his game against Velimirovic from Havana 1971. That game, while instructive, is *nothing* like Liren's masterpiece! Quite the contrary. But it has something in common: the a-pawn. In the article Donner wrote a 3rd person 'letter' from his king addressed to his a-pawn, the hero, the 'Sweet Little Thing' of the article's title. It struck me that were Donner alive today Liren's game would have sparked another such 'letter to the a-pawn' from him, albeit with a much different tone. Though I make no claims to being Donner's equal with quill and ink, I humbly submit my own 'letter'.

Bai Jinshi-Ding Liren
final position

Sad Little Thing

Letter to *a* Pawn
Dear Albert,
I expected more from you. Anything! Each of your brethren contributed

something to the war effort. Some more than others. Diana's heroic charge, for instance. She swallowed her fear and trekked deep into enemy territory, breaching their front gate almost singlehandedly, striking confusion and discord among their ranks. It was breathtaking. She even felled a

Write to us
New In Chess, P.O. Box 1093
1810 KB Alkmaar, The Netherlands
or e-mail: editors@newinchess.com
Letters may be edited or abridged

knight – a *knight* – before finally meeting her end at the hands of the 'Lady in White.' A tough loss! She would have made a fine queen – nearly did, in fact! Oh yes, that... I know the sudden loss of our queen was weighing heavy on your heart. We all felt that sting, none more than I. But what did *you* do to avenge her? Nothing! I know you are weak, even among those of your rank, but is that an excuse when your comrades are being cut to ribbons around you? Bradly, Curtis, Diane, Emily, Frank and George; one by one they fell on the battlefield, honourably. And what of your twin brother, Harry? Weakling among weaklings he nonetheless burst forth unto the breach like Vysotsky's horses toward the abyss, fearing not for his own safety and even engaging the enemy king directly (to his end), but with noble cause. I hear they are writing songs about him! You alone remain, Albert, sole survivor among my foot soldiers; unscathed, clean, polished armour. Perhaps you thought I would not notice, what with the symphony-like gallantry displayed by our knights; and our archers raining down mayhem from their turrets. Even the clergy took to metal, wielding their crosiers like halberds. What inspiration! And yes, even I – aged and ailing as I am – took to arms facing the enemy king in the final showdown. I marveled at his approach. A worthy

king, I thought, a brave warrior coming to meet his end eyes open, sword drawn. In his honour I had even prepared a royal death, to be delivered swiftly at the hands of my greatest knight, Sir Galavant the Black! But my admiration soon turned to disgust. As the *coup de grâce* was about to be delivered the hapless king suddenly slumped to his knees, his drapes runneth yellow, bawling and pleading for his life. It was horrible. How could he deny me the final movement in my symphony, the final brush stroke to my masterpiece? I thought to quarter and feed him to the swine, but it would not do. No, death is too good for such cowardliness. Such a 'King' must live on to rule in mockery. And in that you are fortunate, dear Albert. Normally I would have simply had you executed. But 'royalty' needs servants, and that you shall be, custodian to the 'royal pot' of your new monarch, the Yellow King, tucked away safely within the bowels of my dungeon.
Sincerely, King

Bruce Monson
Colorado Springs, CO, USA

COLOPHON

PUBLISHER: Allard Hoogland
EDITOR-IN-CHIEF:
Dirk Jan ten Geuzendam
HONORARY EDITOR: Jan Timman
CONTRIBUTING EDITOR: Anish Giri
EDITORS: Peter Boel, René Olthof
ART-DIRECTION: Jan Scholtus
PRODUCTION: Joop de Groot
TRANSLATORS: Ken Neat, Piet Verhagen
SALES AND ADVERTISING: Remmelt Otten

PHOTOS AND ILLUSTRATIONS IN THIS ISSUE:
Maria Emelianova, Eteri Kublashvili, Berend Vonk,
Lennart Ootes, Ole Kristian Strøm
COVER PHOTO: New In Chess

© No part of this magazine may be reproduced,
stored in a retrieval system or transmitted in any
form or by any means, recording or otherwise,
without the prior permission of the publisher.

NEW IN CHESS
P.O. BOX 1093
1810 KB ALKMAAR
THE NETHERLANDS

PHONE: 00-31-(0)72-51 27 137
SUBSCRIPTIONS: nic@newinchess.com
EDITORS: editors@newinchess.com
ADVERTISING: otten@newinchess.com

WWW.NEWINCHESS.COM

The Kings of Their Countries

Last month, Peter Svidler captured his eighth Russian national championship. That is the most that any player has won in Russia, but it is not a record for national championships. Carlos Juárez has reportedly been crowned champion of Guatamala 25 times and Ortvin Sarapu won or tied for first in New Zealand's championship 20 times. The following graphic looks at the players who have won the most open titles (as opposed to women's championships) in some of the strongest chess-playing countries. *DYLAN LOEB McCLAIN*

YEARS OF TITLES (Includes ties for first)

13 NETHERLANDS **Max Euwe**
| 1921 | 1924 | 1926 | 1929 | 1933 | 1938 | 1939 | 1942 | 1947 | 1948 | 1950 | 1952 | 1955 |

12 ITALY **Stefano Tatai**
| 1962 | 1965 | 1967 | 1970 | 1974 | 1977 | 1979 | 1983 | 1985 | 1990 | 1991 | 1995 |

11 ICELAND **Hannes Stefánsson**
| 1998 | 1999 | 2001 | 2002 | 2003 | 2004 | 2005 | 2006 | 2007 | 2008 | 2013 |

SWEDEN **Erik Lundin**
| 1931* | 1932* | 1934* | 1938* | 1941 | 1942 | 1945 | 1946 | 1960 | 1961 | 1964 |

EAST GERMANY **Wolfgang Uhlmann**
| 1954 | 1955 | 1958 | 1964 | 1968 | 1975 | 1976 | 1981 | 1983 | 1985 | 1986 |

◀ *Uhlmann dominated East Germany for decades.*

10 BRITAIN **Jonathan Penrose**
| 1958 | 1959 | 1960 | 1961 | 1962 | 1963 | 1966 | 1967 | 1968 | 1969 |

Penrose abruptly quit playing in 1970, but he went on to become a correspondence grandmaster.

8 RUSSIA **Peter Svidler**
| 1994 | 1995 | 1997 | 2003 | 2008 | 2011 | 2013 | 2017 |

UNITED STATES **Samuel Reshevsky**
| 1936 | 1938 | 1940 | 1941 | 1942 | 1946 | 1957 | 1969 | ◀

Reshevsky would undoubtedly have won more if not for Bobby Fischer.

UNITED STATES **Bobby Fischer**
| 1958 | 1959 | 1960 | 1961 | 1963 | 1964 | 1966 | 1967 |

HUNGARY **Gedeon Barcza**
| 1942 | 1943 | 1947 | 1950 | 1951 | 1955 | 1957 | 1966 |

HUNGARY **Laszlo Szabo**
| 1935 | 1937 | 1939 | 1946 | 1950 | 1952 | 1954 | 1959 |

HUNGARY **Lajos Portisch**
| 1958 | 1961 | 1962 | 1964 | 1965 | 1971 | 1975 | 1981 | ◀

Portisch is one of four players to have won eight Hungarian titles.

HUNGARY **Zoltan Almasi**
| 1995 | 1997 | 1999 | 2000 | 2003 | 2006 | 2008 | 2009 |

FRANCE **Etienne Bacrot**
| 1999 | 2000 | 2001 | 2002 | 2003 | 2008 | 2012 | 2017 |

SPAIN **Miguel Illescas**
| 1995 | 1998 | 1999 | 2001 | 2004 | 2005 | 2007 | 2010 | ◀

CANADA **Daniel Yanofsky**
| 1941 | 1943 | 1945 | 1947 | 1953 | 1959 | 1963 | 1965 |

Illescas's last title broke a tie with Antonio Medina and Arturo Pomar.

* The championship was unofficial before 1939.

Garry Kasparov: 'Trump has a very thin skin, a condition I admit that I share.'
(The former world champion-turned-political activist, commenting on the controversial US president in The Weekly Standard)

Lawrence Trent: 'I just spent the morning coaching kids – and I estimate this will save me tens of thousands of dollars, as now I don't want to have any!'
(Interviewed by Maurice Ashley during the London Chess Classic. In the morning, he'd led an overcrowded LCC coaching session for school kids)

Brough Scott: 'Polo is galloping chess.'
(The long-standing British horse racing journalist, speaking in early December on BBC Radio 4's flagship news programme, Today)

Norman Reedus: 'I taught Mingus to play [chess] when he was young. We'd come here, play game after game, and I'd watch him beat people in minutes. And I'd think, "That's my kid!"'
(The Walking Dead cult star, as he meets up with his lookalike young model son, Mingus, outside Washington Square Park in New York for the season two finale of his AMC biker travelogue series, RIDE)

Peter Heine Nielsen: 'The Russian Chess Championship is played by 12 players. And in the end Peter Svidler always wins.'
(Tweeted by Magnus Carlsen's trainer, as he mimicked Gary Lineker's famous quote about the Germans and football)

Maxime Vachier-Lagrave: 'Chess preserves a state of youthful grace that allows us to prolong our childhood.' *(From MVL's recently published French book, Joueur d'échecs – reviewed in this issue by Matthew Sadler)*

Lord Hope of Craighead: 'Prosecuting is like a game of chess, you have no time to be squeamish.'
(One of the UK's most distinguished legal minds, quoted in The Times in early December on life as a top lawyer before going on to become a Supreme Court judge)

Dr. John Sharples: 'The chessplayer is a performer of a kind of secular magic, sharing enchanted links with the conjuror and circus-performer.' *(The academic author in his new book for Manchester University Press, A Cultural History of Chess-Players: Minds, machines and monsters)*

Tyler Cowen: 'In chess, computers show that what we call "strategy" is reducible to tactics, ultimately. It only looks creative to us. They are still just glorified cash registers. This should make us feel uncomfortable, whether or not we think computers will ever be good composers of music or artistic painters.' *(The American economist talking on the growth of AI)*

Vladimir Kramnik: 'I think that Lasker is the discoverer of modern chess. When you look at Steinitz's games, they have a very 19th-century feel ... Lasker had many games that could be played by any modern player.'
(A fitting tribute from one world champion to another, as 2018 heralds in the 150th anniversary of Emanuel Lasker's birth)

Charles Krauthammer: 'Chess is a particularly enclosed, self-referential activity. It's not just that it lacks the fresh air of sports, but that it lacks connection to the real world outside – a tether to reality enjoyed by the monomaniacal students of other things, say volcanic ash or the mating habits of the tsetse fly.' *(The US political commentator, author, columnist and chess fanatic)*

Frank Herbert: 'Logic is good for playing chess but is often too slow for the needs of survival.'
(The sci-fi writer in Chapterhouse: Dune, the sixth and final novel in his cult Dune Chronicles)

Anatol Rapoport: 'One cannot play chess if one becomes aware of the pieces as living souls and of the fact that the Whites and the Blacks have more in common with each other than with the players.' *(The Russian-born American mathematical psychologist, 1911-2007, in his book Strategy and Conscience)*

Carlsen overall winner Grand Chess Tour

Caruana clinches London Classic

After five rounds he was a comfortable full point ahead of the pack. Nothing seemed to indicate that Fabiano Caruana would need a last-round Houdini act and a blitz play-off to edge out Ian Nepomniachtchi. But when those moments came, the world number two was up to the task. The London Classic was also the final leg of the 2017 Grand Chess Tour. In the last round a struggling Magnus Carlsen managed to turn around a dubious position against Aronian to win the GCT, raising his total tour earnings to a grand total of $245,350.

DIRK JAN TEN GEUZENDAM

Good form is a fickle mistress. She comes and goes as she pleases. Excellent company while she is there, but leaving you nonplussed when she suddenly leaves again. Fabiano Caruana knows all about it. After his win at the London Classic the American grandmaster looked back on a year that he called 'overall pretty bad'. 'I was struggling quite a lot throughout the year and there were some complete disasters, such as Paris, the US Championship and the Sinquefield Cup.'

A partial explanation was the permanent concern he felt about his rating, as he had decided to skip the FIDE Grand Prix and hoped to qualify for the Candidates' tournament on rating. 'Right after I had beaten Kramnik in the first round in the Isle of Man and more or less secured that spot, that took a lot of pressure off of me.'

And once he felt carefree again, he ended a year that he had already pretty much written off with two huge successes. 'I am not even sure if London is a bigger achievement for me, because beating Grischuk in a blitz and rapid match (at the Champions Showdown in St. Louis) is also something that I am very proud of.

Fabiano Caruana: 'Winning this kind of tournament is very much down to specific details. It may come down to playing the right opponent on the right day, or choosing the right opening against the right opponent.'

Somewhere in the middle of the
match I thought, this is over. Things
started falling apart. The third day
I was losing games, I was getting
outplayed and I was also blundering a lot. But somehow I pulled it
together and he started to feel shaky.
The tide turned and Day 4 was pretty
one-sided.'

Doomsday atmosphere

In London, Caruana's first game was
immediately one of the key moments.
'It was of massive importance that I
didn't lose that long game against
Magnus. I was being outplayed
from the opening and I was playing
Magnus in a type of position in which
he is usually deadly.'

The draw against Carlsen was one
of five draws in the first round, and
in Rounds 2 and 3, all games were
drawn as well. Nothing wildly excep-
tional for an elite event, but for some
reason the absence of decisive games
in the first couple of rounds created a
Doomsday atmosphere at the Classic,
and for days the live broadcast had an
annoying focus on the draw death of
chess.

Looking at the games in question,
various explanations could be given,
but in this case a look at the tournament schedule might also suggest
one. The Classic began with a 'Pro
Biz' event that started at 10 in the
morning and from which the players
didn't get back till 9 in the evening.
The next day they were taken to the
futuristic Google DeepMind head-
quarters for the first round. Having
one round at 'Google' had considerable implications for the rest of the
schedule. Immediately after the first
round there was a free day and, as a
consequence, the final round was
played on a Monday, which meant
that on the day that the prizes were
divided, the Olympia conference
centre was practically deserted, a
weird scene for anyone who knows
the masses of chess enthusiasts that
normally fill the place and make the
Classic such a great event to go to.

Caruana confessed that after the
first two days he already felt burnt
out, but that he managed to stabilize
pretty well. 'And things also went in
my favour. I think winning this kind
of tournament is very much down to
specific details. It may come down to
playing the right opponent on the right
day, or choosing the right opening
against the right opponent. You can
only know if these things were correct
or incorrect with hindsight.'

Having beaten Karjakin and Anand
in Rounds 4 and 5, Caruana had a
one-point lead over the rest and was
the favourite for first prize until Ian
Nepomniachtchi leapfrogged him
with a hat-trick in Rounds 6 to 8.

And so, when 'Nepo' made a quick
draw with White against Vachier-
Lagrave in the last round, it was clear
that Caruana had to beat Michael
Adams to force a play-off. After the
opening the Englishman didn't look
like the right opponent on the right
day, but in the end he turned out to be
that opponent after all.

**Fabiano Caruana
Michael Adams**
London 2017 (9)

position after 32.♔g1

White has just played his third
'aimless' king move in a row. If Black
continues to shuffle around, doing
nothing either, it is hard to see how
White can make any progress. His
extra pawn in the 'Irish Pawn Centre'
on the e-file is of little use. But Adams
plays a move that allows Caruana to
keep the game going.
32...♖d5 33.♖c4 ♖a5 34.♖c2

The rook has to go back, since Black can meet 34.♖f4 with 34...g5! when, after 35.♖f6 ♘xe5 36.♘xe5 ♖xe5, there are no white threats on the f-file, while Black is close to winning pawns here and there and winning the game. But Caruana had seen a 'trick'.

34...♗d5 35.♘d4 ♘xd4 36.exd4 ♖g3

37.♖f3! Black may have counted on 37.♖f2 or 37.e3, when in a tense position he gets attacking chances, but this is different.

37...♗xf3 38.exf3 c6 39.♔h2 ♖xg2+ 40.♔xg2 And suddenly White is up a pretty healthy pawn, an advantage that Caruana converted into a win (1-0, 68).

While Caruana was working for hours to beat Adams, Nepomniachtchi was in his hotel room, resting and preparing for a possible play-off. Caruana secured the play-off but seemed at a clear disadvantage, since he barely had time to adjust to facing one of the fastest GMs on the planet. In the first two games (10 minutes with a 5-second 'delay') 'Nepo' had the initiative, but both games ended in a draw. The craziest game, as they continued with 5 minutes and a 3-second delay, was the third one, in which the Russian blundered a full piece but continued as if nothing had happened and miraculously managed to draw. And then Caruana won Game 4.

He had managed to keep some energy in reserve, and it was only now that he suddenly felt completely

wiped out. And happy. 'I wasn't thinking of my chances. I already felt as if I had achieved my main goal, which was shared tournament victory, and I worked very hard for this final point. And we weren't playing for money, so it was basically for bragging rights. But I did want to win. I wasn't trying to put too much pressure on myself, which probably worked out for the best.'

When we asked the winner of the 2017 London Chess Classic to annotate one of his wins, he chose the game that proved to be a turning point in his tournament.

NOTES BY
Fabiano Caruana

Fabiano Caruana
Vishy Anand
London 2017 (5)
Four Knights Opening

The day before this game, I had beaten Sergey Karjakin and broken clear of the field. Every other game had been drawn, and fans were again calling it the death of chess prematurely, as it turned out, since the tournament ended with a lot of wild, decisive games and one of the closest play-off finishes possible. I was in an ambitious mood before this game, but considering my recent score against Vishy, I also wanted to stay relatively cautious.

1.e4 e5 2.♘f3 ♘c6 3.♗b5 ♘f6 4.d3 ♗c5 5.♘c3

I recently played this move in the rapid/blitz match against Alexander Grischuk during the Champions Showdown in St. Louis, reaching clearly worse positions out of the opening twice and losing both games. Normally, I would immediately chuck the entire line, but I decided to try my luck with it once again.

5...0-0 6.♗xc6 dxc6 7.h3

This move is often played to discourage ...♗g4, or just because players don't have much better to do, but playing it before castling signals my intention to attack on the kingside with g4.

7.♘xe5!? is a move with an interesting history. It was played by Magnus Carlsen almost a decade ago, and since then not a single player within 1000 points of his rating has dared to repeat it, which surprises me, because it's not a bad move at all.

7...♘d7 8.♗e3 ♗d6 9.♘e2

First preparing the knight swing to g3.

9...♖e8 10.g4

Engines are so critical of this plan, generally, that when analysing this line it's a better idea to just turn the computer off.

10...♘c5 11.♘g3 ♘e6 12.♘f5 c5 13.h4

13...a5 This is an interesting moment. It feels very natural for Black to play ...♘d4, but with the queen on d1 that loses a lot of its bite, and saves White some valuable time for c3. So both players are making as many useful moves as possible before the move ♕d2, after which ...♘d4 gains significantly in strength.
13...♘d4?! 14.c3 ♘xf3+ 15.♕xf3 gives White a big head start on the attack.
14.h5 ♖a6 This move surprised me slightly. Vishy probably wanted the rook to be defensively placed on the sixth rank in case something should happen on the kingside. It also makes sense in some lines to have the pawn on a5, where it supports a ♗b4 pin on the queen on d2.
I had been expecting 14...a4 first.

15.♕d2?!
This was a difficult decision, and not one I really wanted to make. After playing it, I immediately regretted being so impatient.
15.c3, preparing ♕d2, is the correct choice. I wasn't sure about the position after 15...♘f4 16.♗xf4 exf4

17.♕d2 ♗e6 18.c4, but it remains very messy and is better than what happened in the game.
15...♘d4 16.♖h3 ♗f8 17.0-0-0 ♗e6 18.♔b1
I still thought I was doing relatively well. I am certainly not better, but I didn't feel like I was worse. Vishy's next move was a cold shower.

18...f6! Calm and correct. Now I was extremely unhappy with my position. I had been expecting 18...♘xf3 19.♖xf3 c4 20.dxc4 ♕xd2 21.♖xd2 ♗xc4, which is an equal ending in a variety of ways. I wasn't opposed to a draw at this stage.
19.c3 ♘xf3
This is a fine choice, but there was an option that also had me worried.
19...♕d7!?, just leaving the knight hanging and going for the attack, deserved attention. Now 20.cxd4 cxd4 21.♗xd4 exd4 22.♘3xd4 ♗f7 is forced, and White faces a difficult decision of how to defend the king, with two bishops, a queen and a rook bearing down on the queenside. I had spent some time calculating and concluded that 23.♕c2 should hold it together.
20.♖xf3

20...c4?! This is a very natural move, but it lets me off the hook somewhat.
20...h6 felt slightly anti-positional to me, but it is very difficult for White to drum up any attack after it. I was counting on 21.♖g3 ♕d7 22.f4, but after 22...exf4 23.♗xf4 ♕f7 24.a3 (24.c4 b5 similarly breaks through) 24...b5 White is forced to sacrifice: 25.♗xh6 gxh6 26.♘xh6+ ♗xh6 27.♕xh6 ♕g7 28.♕f4 ♗g5, and the attack has clearly failed.
21.♕c2
21.dxc4? looks almost playable, until you notice a crucial detail at the end: 21...♗xf5 22.♕xd8 (22.gxf5 ♖d6 skewers the queen and rook) 22...♗xe4+ 23.♔c1 ♖xd8 24.♖xd8 ♗xf3 25.♗c5 ♖d6! and oops, the skewer is intercepted.
21.g5 was probably better than what I played, and I hesitated between the two options, but finally I decided ♕c2 looks more natural.
21...cxd3 22.♖xd3 ♕c8 23.g5

At this point my decisions were easy, because my position was strategically dubious, so I had to play very concretely.
23...fxg5 24.♗xg5

Fabiano Caruana's win against Vishy Anand proved to be a turning point: 'Engines are so critical of this plan that when analysing this line it's better to just turn the computer off.'

24...♗f7?! The only move I had considered, but also an inaccuracy. Vishy was probably not too concerned about h6 gxh6, as his king looks very safe, but as we will see, it can still come under attack.

24...h6! 25.♗c1 ♗f7 26.♖g3 looks like counterplay, but after 26...♔h7 it turns out the counterplay is an illusion, and the pawn on h5 is dropping off.

25.h6 It took some time to decide on this, because my position still looked very bad, until I saw my next move.

25...gxh6

26.♗c1! My best move of the game. The bishop looks as if it will automatically go to e3, but instead it will find its place on b2, where it acts as both a defender and an attacker.

After 26.♗e3 Black goes 26...b5, and next ...♕e6 will put White under strong pressure.

26...♕e6 27.b3 a4 This feels too direct, and my play becomes much easier. Vishy mentioned 27...b5!? as an improvement after the game. It was what I was most worried about, and I had planned 28.♘e3, with the idea of possibly bringing the knight to d5. White is definitely not better, but remains fully in the game.

28.c4 Now I was already confident I wouldn't lose, but I could hardly have expected to win this position in 10 moves.

28...axb3 29.axb3

29...♕c6 29...♖ea8?! 30.♗b2, and White's king is completely secure. The same cannot be said for Black's.

30.♖g3+ ♔h8
The king doesn't want to go on this diagonal, but ...♗g6 will be met by ♖d5, so there was no choice.

31.♖d1
This was also a tough decision, because f3 has its pluses as well, but I was low on time and decided to be practical and trust my intuition.

31...b5 32.c5
32.cxb5?? ♖a1+ is best avoided. However, 32.♗b2!? was an option, leading to a messy position after 32...bxc4 33.♖d8 ♖a5!.

32...b4? A very serious mistake, but surprisingly I was expecting it. Black is ambitiously preparing ...♖a5, which would be a good idea if it weren't for a tactical shot.

Black should have played 32...♕xc5 33.♕xc5 ♗xc5 34.♖d7, and it looks like White has the initiative, but after 34...♗g6 35.♗xh6 ♗f8 it all turns into a drawish ending.

33.♗b2

33...♗g6 This doesn't put up much resistance, but the position is already atrocious for Black.

At this point I think Vishy realized that 33...♖a5 would run into 34.♖d8!.

I was trying to calculate the consequences of this during the game, and failed to find a forced win, but it is certainly winning: 34...♕xc5 35.♖xe8 ♗xe8 36.f4! ♗g6 37.fxe5!. This is the critical move, rather than the more natural ♗xe5. 37...♔g8 38.e6 ♕xc2+ 39.♔xc2 ♗d6 40.♖f3 ♗xf5 41.exf5, and White's pawns are unstoppable. The other alternative, 33...♕xc5 34.♕xc5 ♗xc5 35.♖d7 ♗g6 36.f4, is very unpleasant, but Black can still continue to resist with 36...♗d6 37.fxe5 ♗xe5 38.♗xe5+ ♖xe5 39.♖d8+ ♗e8 (39...♖e8? 40.♖xg6 wins a piece because of the loose rook on a6) 40.♘g7 ♖xe4 41.♖xe8+ ♖xe8 42.♘xe8, and judging by some recent games, these piece-up positions can be pretty tough to win.

34.♖d5

Now it's hard to imagine Black holding it all together. Some of the following moves are questionable, but I felt pretty sure I would win.

34...♕b5 35.♖g1 c6 36.♖xe5 ♖xe5 37.♗xe5+ ♔g8 38.♗d4 ♔f7 39.♘h4 Black resigned.

■ ■ ■

As much as Caruana looked like the big favourite after five rounds, Ian Nepomniachtchi held the best cards with one round to go. Two windfalls and a hard-fought game propelled the Russian into the lead. Against Adams he won an equal endgame that the Englishman would have drawn on most other days, and in the penultimate round Carlsen suddenly started drifting and almost forced his own defeat with a couple of shocking oversights.

In-between Nepomniachtchi won a good game against Vishy Anand, who had a hard time in London.

NOTES BY
Ian Nepomniachtchi

Ian Nepomniachtchi
Vishy Anand
London 2017 (7)
English Opening

1.c4 ♘f6 2.♘c3 e6
Vishy normally prefers ...e5, but the previous day the game Anand-Karjakin was played, and the comfortable equality in one of the sharp lines, demonstrated by Sergey, probably appealed to my opponent, so that this move did not come as a great surprise.

3.♘f3 d5 4.e3 a6!?
An ambitious plan. 4...c5 or 4...♗e7 more often occur.

5.b3 As long as the pawn remains on d2, the bishop on the long diagonal makes a pleasing impression.

5...♗d6
5...c5 6.♗b2 ♘c6 seems more logical to me, but Black, at the least, is consistent.

6.♗b2 0-0 7.g4!?

Knocking the puck into the danger zone! I had planned this new move in advance and I made it quite quickly. Even with the pawn on c6 the g2-g4-g5 advance is considered quite thematic, and in this version, with the d5-pawn hanging, White is able to get by without loss of material.

7...♘xg4 I think that Black has to choose the critical course, since neither 7...♘c6 8.g5 ♘e4 9.♖g1 nor 7...dxc4 8.g5 ♘fd7 9.♗xc4 ♘c6 10.♘e4 looks like a worthy alternative. In both cases White has a highly promising initiative.

8.♖g1 f5 The weakening of the e6-square favours White.
8...♘f6 would also have led to unclear play: 9.cxd5 e5 10.♕c2 ♗g4 11.♘g5 ♗h5 12.♗d3. A detailed analysis of the resulting positions could take up all of the New Year holidays, so I will offer to the judgement of the reader only some sample variations: 12...g6 13.♘ce4 ♘xd5 (13...♘bd7 14.♘g3 gives White an initiative) 14.♗c4 ♘b6 15.♘xh7 ♔xh7 16.♘g5+ ♔h6 17.♗e2! ♕e8 (17...♕xg5 loses to 18.♖xg5 ♔xg5 19.f4+) 18.♗xh5 ♔xh5!? (following the precepts of Steinitz) 19.f4 ♘8d7 20.0-0-0 ♔h6 21.f5 ♔g7 22.d4 with compensation for the piece.

9.cxd5 e5 10.h3 ♘f6 11.♘g5 ♕e7 12.♕f3
The alternative was 12.♘e6 ♗xe6 13.dxe6 ♘c6 14.♕f3, denying Black an additional option on the 12th move.

12...♔h8

Vishy did not give in to the obvious provocation, although this possibly deserved attention: 12...e4 13.♕g2 ♘bd7 14.0-0-0 (14.♘e6 ♖f7 is not so terrible) 14...♘e5 15.d3 ♘xd3+ 16.♗xd3 exd3 17.♖xd3 g6 18.h4 ♗d7 19.♔b1 ♖ae8 20.f3 with the initiative for White.

13.♘e6

13...♗xe6

It is unlikely that anyone would venture 13...♖g8!? 14.♕xf5 c6 15.f4 (15.e4 cxd5 16.exd5 ♘c6!) 15...cxd5 16.fxe5 ♗xe5 17.♕xe5 ♗xe6 18.♘e2 ♘c6 19.♕g5 when the dark-squared bishop is eyeing the opponent's kingside just too intently.

And after 13...♖f7 14.♕xf5 ♘xd5 15.♘xd5 ♕xe6 16.♕xe6 ♗xe6 17.♗c4, in order not to lose immediately, Black has to find 17...♖a7 18.♘b6 ♗xc4 19.♘xc4 ♘c6 20.♔e2 ♖a8 21.♖af1 ♔g8 22.f4.

14.dxe6 ♕xe6

14...♘c6 15.♕xf5, and the two bishops guarantee White a comfortable advantage.

15.♕xb7 ♘bd7

16.♗c4?!

A blank shot. The bishop will not be able to stay long on c4, whereas e7 is the right place for the black queen: the possible exchange of the dark-squared bishops will make Black's life significantly easier, and it will not harm the g7-point to have an additional defender.

16.0-0-0 ♕e7 17.♔b1 ♗a3 18.♗a1 ♘b6 was possibly over-optimistic, but the cool-headed 16.♕xa6 e4 17.♗c4 ♕e8 deserved attention:

A) 18.♕b5 ♖b8 19.♕xf5 ♘e5 and Black has compensation for the pawns;

B) 18.♘b5 ♕e7 19.♘xd6 ♕xd6 20.♕d5 ♕xd5 21.♗xd5 ♘xd5 22.♗xg7+ ♔g8 23.♗xf8+ ♔xf8 24.♖g5 ♘e7, and the black cavalry will have numerous favourable outposts;

C) 18.♕c6 ♖b8 19.f4 exf3 20.♕xf3 ♘e5 21.♕g2 ♕e7 22.♗e2, and Black does not have sufficient compensation for the pawn.

16...♕e7 17.♕g2 ♘b6 18.♗e2 a5

19.♗b5

The bishop at last finds its place in life. 19.♕g5?! is unsuitable: 19...a4 20.♖c1 (both after 20.♕xf5 a3 21.♗c1 e4 and 20.bxa4 ♖xa4 21.♘xa4 ♖xa4 Black is slightly better) 20...axb3 21.axb3 g6 22.h4 ♕e6 23.h5 ♖g8 as this position favours Black.

19...♖ad8

The black pieces are excellently placed, but the two bishops and slightly better pawn structure allow White to remain optimistic.

20.♕g5

Celeb 64

John Henderson

Sandrine Bonnaire

Sandrine Bonnaire is that rare breed of French actresses who became a star without ever having teased moviegoers with that coquettish guess-who-I-really-am sort of reserve. Ms. Bonnaire made her first big splash at 16, playing a Parisian schoolgirl in the film *A Nos Amours* (1983). As good as her debut was, what really impressed was her later starring role in Caroline Bottaro's chess-themed movie *Queen to Play* (2009), adapted from the novel *La joueuse d'échecs* by Bertina Henrichs. In this grown-up fairytale, Ms. Bonnaire plays Cinderella hotel maid Hélène, who, after seeing a couple engage in some seriously, sexually tense chess on their hotel balcony, decides to take up the game in the hope of rekindling her dreary marriage. She finds a mentor in a man (Kevin Kline) she works for. He trains her, patiently honing her strategy and insights into the game, which turns out to be a convenient lesson in life. And as she improves, she joins a chess club and prepares for her first tournament – but what was sublime was how Ms. Bonnaire played the part, going from a beginner initially fumbling with the pieces, to confidently flicking them around the board while pressing her clock without missing a beat. Small wonder. Ms. Bonnaire is a method actor who totally immerses herself in each role she plays – so just as in the movie, she took lessons at her local chess club and also played in a minor tournament. ■

20...g6

Despite the weakening of the long diagonal, this is the most solid move. The possible alternative does not look too clear: 20...f4 21.0-0-0 h6 22.♕g6 ♗a3 23.♗xa3 ♕xa3+ 24.♔b1 ♕e7 25.exf4 e4 26.f3 exf3 27.♖de1 ♕f7 28.♕xf7 ♖xf7 29.♖gf1 ♖xd2 30.♖xf3.

21.♕h6 ♘g8 22.♕g5 ♘f6

Anand sensibly avoids the exchange of queens, since without active counterplay the queenside pawns will become a convenient target for the white pieces.

23.♖d1

Overcoming the irresistible desire to repeat moves, White vacates the a1-square for his bishop and looks for an active plan.

23...e4?!

Vishy insists on the exchange of the dark-squared bishops, but now the c3-knight comes very strongly into play. The dynamic balance would have been retained after, for example, 23...♕e6 or 23...♗b4.

24.♕h6 ♖g8 25.♘e2 ♗e5 26.♗xe5 ♕xe5 27.♘f4

I was aiming for this position when I played 23.♖d1.

Ian Nepomniachtchi waits for Vishy Anand to make his next opening move. Soon the Russian will 'knock the puck into the danger zone!'

27...g5!

Out of two evils Black chooses the lesser.

27...♕xb5 28.♘xg6+ ♖xg6 29.♖xg6 ♖g8 30.♖xg8+ ♘xg8 31.♕e6 ♕c5 32.f3!? (32.d3 exd3 33.♖xd3 ♔g7 and it would appear that Black will succeed in coordinating his pieces) 32...exf3 33.♔f2 was passive, but resilient enough:

A) 33...♘e7 34.♕f6+ ♔g8 35.h4 ♕b5 36.d3 is better for White;

B) 33...f4 34.♖g1 (34.♔xf3 fxe3 35.dxe3 ♕h5+ 36.♕g4 ♕f7+) 34...fxe3+ 35.dxe3 ♕f8, with a defensible position.

28.♖xg5 ♖xg5 29.♕xg5 ♖g8 30.♕h6

30...♖g7? A strange choice. Black needed to play more enterprisingly: 30...♖g1+ 31.♗f1 ♘bd7 32.♘e2 ♖g6 33.♕h4 (33.♕f4 ♘d5! 34.♕xe5+ ♘xe5 35.♘d4 c5 36.♘xf5 ♘f3+ 37.♔e2 ♘g1+ with a perpetual) 33...♕d6.

ANALYSIS DIAGRAM

The activity of the black pieces should be sufficient for equality.

31.♗c4 Now in the event of a check the king will simply move to e2.

31...♘xc4

The mass exchanges after 31...♘fd5 32.♔e2 ♘xc4 33.bxc4 ♘xf4+ 34.♕xf4 ♕c5 35.d3 are, alas, no panacea.

32.bxc4 ♕b2 33.♔e2 a4 34.♘e6

The over-hasty 34.♖b1? ♕xb1 35.♕xf6 h6! would have thrown away the advantage.

34...♖f7

35.♘f4 Here I had almost decided on 35.♘d8 ♖g7 36.♖g1, but I noticed in time the saving 36...♘g4! 37.hxg4 ♕c2. Of course, here also White has an enormous advantage, but the position no longer looks so solid: 38.f4 ♕d3+ (38...exf3+ 39.♔xf3 fxg4+ 40.♔e2 ♕xc4+ 41.♔d1, winning) 39.♔e1 ♕xd8 40.♕e6 ♕h4+ 41.♔d1 fxg4 42.f5.

35...♖g7 36.a3

White prevents the ...a4-a3 advance and slightly improves on the idea of the previous variation.

36...♘e8

After 36...c5 Black is not helped by the idea of blocking the g-file: 37.♘e6 ♖f7 38.♘d8 ♖g7 39.♖g1 ♘g4 40.♕d6 and wins.

It was possible to resist with 36...♕b6 37.d3 ♕b2+ 38.♖d2 ♕c3 39.♘e6 ♖g2 40.♕h4 ♔g8 41.dxe4 ♕xc4+ 42.♔f3 ♖g6 43.♖d8+ ♔f7 44.♘g5+ ♔g7 45.♖d4 ♕c6 although White is of course much better here.

37.♕c6

White eliminates the dangerous pawn. The rest is a matter of straightforward technique, which my opponent preferred not to test.
Black resigned.

∎ ∎ ∎

With his sudden collapse against his friend Nepomniachtchi, Magnus Carlsen hit rock-bottom in London. Suffering from a nasty cold, he had been unable to play a prominent role, and now even his overall win in the Grand Chess Tour, which for a long time had seemed a forgone conclusion, was suddenly in jeopardy. With one round to go, Maxime Vachier-Lagrave could overtake him if everything went well for the Frenchman on the final day.

Carlsen was in a foul mood and barely managed to speak when he appeared in front of the camera together with Maurice Ashley after his loss to Nepomniachtchi. He even lost his temper when the show host kindly tried to adjust his collar before they went on air, throwing his arms in the air and angrily telling him not to touch him.

But on the last day he showed his fighting spirit when he survived a dubious position against Levon Aronian and looked for more when he was offered a draw. At that point, a draw was enough to win the tour, as MVL had made a quick draw, but now Carlsen wanted more, and he got it.

For Vachier-Lagrave it was a fitting end for a year in which he missed qualifying for the Candidates by a hair's breadth no fewer than three times. Again it was close, and again no cigar. Nevertheless he confirmed

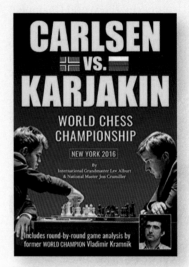

time and again that he is one of the very best players in the world, and no doubt he found further consolation in his total earnings in the 2017 GCT: $ 207,917. Not exactly a measly amount.

When Magnus Carlsen was handed the trophy by tournament director Malcolm Pein, the World Champion managed a smile again. He thanked each and every person present, showing his sense of humour when he added 'including those who hate me.'

We'll round off with the effort that brought back his smile, with notes by his second, Peter Heine Nielsen.

NOTES BY
Peter Heine Nielsen

Levon Aronian
Magnus Carlsen
London 2017 (9)
Old Benoni Defence

Magnus Carlsen and Maxime Vachier-Lagrave went into the last round in a neck-and-neck race fighting for overall victory in the Grand Chess Tour. Magnus was leading by three Grand Prix points, but Maxime had half a point more in the tournament. Scenarios like we have seen in the Olympiad, where games not involving the contenders for first prize decide on the outcome, had become possible. For instance, it was unclear whether, if MVL drew against Nepomniachtchi – as in fact happened – Magnus would need a draw or a win in his game against Aronian. True to style, the World Champion decided to take fate in his own hands and went for a complicated battle.

1.d4 e6!?
Inviting the French, but mainly trying to create a bit of confusion.
2.♘f3 c5
And now inviting a Sicilian after 3.e4!?. Aronian tries to keep the ball

in 'his' court, keeping a d4-based structure.
3.g3 cxd4 4.♘xd4 ♕b6!? 5.♗g2 ♗c5

Magnus's play is provocative, but there is definitely logic in it, so it comes as no surprise that Bent Larsen actually already played this back in 1968! Attacking the knight on d4 before White has castled and f2 is protected means that White has to make a defensive move.
6.e3 d5
Larsen played 6...♘c6 against Pomar and went on to win the game.
7.♕g4!? Aronian joins the fun, replicating Black's concept of using his queen to provoke weaknesses by exploiting his lack of development.
7.0-0 or 7.c4 would lead to more normal positions.

7...♗f8!
7...g6 would indeed weaken the dark squares and turn later castling into a much more risky affair. So, while obviously not developing looks strange, 8...♘f6 comes next, winning some of the lost time back.
8.0-0 ♘f6 9.♕e2 e5!?
In principle, only this move is a

'The World Champion decided to take fate in his own hands and went for a complicated battle.'

novelty, as 9...♗d7 was played here in the 2013 Finnish Championship in Salo-Lehtinen.

10.♕b5+ ♗d7 11.♕xb6 axb6 12.♘b3 ♘c6
Black actually got a fine position out of the opening and has equalized. But now he hits on a wrong plan, which Aronian duly exploits.
13.♗d2

13...♗d6?!
Stockfish, whose authority has obviously been put in doubt by the alien-like performance of AlphaZero, suggests 13...h5 14♘c3 ♗e6 here, which at least to a human looks perfectly sensible. Instead, Black now drifts into passivity.
14.♘c3 ♗e7 15.a4!

Touching exactly Black's weak spot. Now ♘b5 cannot be prevented, and if ...♗b8, there follows ♗b4. This leaves Black only with the sad game continuation.

15...0-0 16.♘b5 ♗xb5 17.axb5 ♖ac8 18.♗c3 h5 19.♖fd1 ♖fd8 20.♘d2

Magnus Carlsen chatting with his second Peter Heine Nielsen before being interviewed in the studio after his last-round win over Levon Aronian. Finally the World Champion managed a smile again.

White has a better pawn structure and the bishop pair, but Black's position is solid. Aronian reroutes his worst placed piece, heading for f3 to attack the white centre.

20...h4 21.♘f3 hxg3 22.hxg3 e4

Conceding the dark squares. 23...♘g6 was possible, but leaves Black with absolutely no counterplay.

23.♘g5 ♘g6 24.♖a7

At this point, MVL's game had ended in a draw, and the other results also seemed to be going Magnus' way, which meant that a draw would be

sufficient to win the Grand Chess Tour. The main problem, however, was the position on the board in front of him.

24...♖b8 25.♗d4 ♗c5

Again, a passive defence was available, but instead of the sad 25...♘d7, Magnus sacrifices a pawn, aiming for some positional compensation.

26.♗xc5 bxc5

27.c4! Breaking up Black's structure, and effectively winning a pawn.

27...♘e7 28.cxd5 ♘c8!

Aiming for d6.

29.♖a4! By attacking e4, Aronian forces Black's knight to make a detour.

29...♘b6 30.♖a3 ♘c4 31.♖c3 ♘d6 32.♖xc5

White has won a pawn, but Black can be somewhat satisfied, since he has stabilized the position. Aronian later stated that he had definitely overestimated his chances here. Although White is still slightly better, he is by no means winning.

32...♖a8 33.♗h3 ♖e8 34.♖c7 ♔f8 35.b6 ♖e5

Aronian's play has been consistent with his optimism. While Magnus now might have trapped the knight at g5, the point was to sacrifice it anyway!

36.♘e6+!? fxe6 37.dxe6

37...♘fe8!

Met with huge relief among the Norwegian supporters, since anything else seemed to lose. And while this move might at first seem illogical because it removes a defender from the kingside, keeping the knight on d6 is what matters most. And as 37...♖d8 would leave Black almost in complete zugzwang, this is the only way!

38.♖d7 ♖aa5

Grand Chess Tour 2017	
Magnus Carlsen	$245,417
Maxime Vachier-Lagrave	$207,917
Levon Aronian	$91,250
Hikaru Nakamura	$77,500
Fabiano Caruana	$95,000
Sergey Karjakin	$75,000
Wesley So	$79,167
Ian Nepomniachtchi	$100,000
Vishy Anand	$75,000
Anish Giri	$15,000
Alexander Grischuk	$15,000
Shakhriyar Mamedyarov	$12,500
Vladimir Kramnik	$11,250
Peter Svidler	$20,000
Leinier Domínguez	$10,000
Le Quang Liem	$10,000
Garry Kasparov	$7,500
Vassily Ivanchuk	$7,500
Veselin Topalov	$7,500
Michael Adams	$15,000
Etienne Bacrot	$7,500
Baadur Jobava	$7,500
David Navara	$7,500

5 legs:
1. Paris rapid & blitz
2. Leuven rapid & blitz
3. St. Louis Sinquefield Cup
4. St. Louis rapid & blitz
5. London Chess Classic

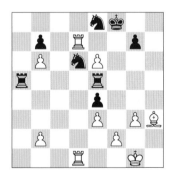

39.b4?

The trend has been bad for Aronian, but it was still possible to save the game. 39.♖1xd6 ♘xd6 40.♖xd6 ♖ad5 41.♖xd5 ♖xd5 42.e7+ ♔xe7 43.♗c8 leads to an easily drawn endgame an exchange down. Now, however, he does cross the line.

39...♖ad5!

Winning instantly, as d6 is now

protected and Black is simply just a piece up.

40.♖a1 ♖b5 41.♖a8 ♖xb6 42.♗g4

Here Aronian offered a draw. His position is lost, but as the tournament result had clarified to the extent that a draw would give Magnus overall victory – and Black is still pinned on the bottom rank – it was not such a bad psychological ploy to put even bigger pressure on his opponent. But Magnus, of course, played on.

42...♖d5! Protecting d6 and getting ready to take on b4.

43.♔g2 ♖xb4 44.♖a1 ♖bb5 45.♗e2 ♖b2 46.♗g4 ♖dd2 47.♔h3 ♖xf2 48.♔h4 ♖h2+ 49.♗h3 g5+ 50.♔h5 ♖xh3+ 51.♔g6 ♖f2 52.e7+ ♔g8 53.♖xd6!

A last trick, since 53...♘xd6?? leads to mate after 54.♖a8+, but obviously Black has numerous defences.

53...♖h7!

The simplest. Next is ...♖g7+ and ...♔f7, leaving Aronian no choice but to resign.

Not Magnus's best game or his best tournament, but it got the job done when it mattered! ■

Game Changer

AlphaZero crushes Stockfish

AlphaZero, a creation of Google subsidiary DeepMind, beat Stockfish 8 by 64 to 36 without losing a game in a one-minute-per-move match on powerful hardware. The crushing defeat sent shockwaves through the chess world and the world at large, not in the last place because AlphaZero had taught itself to play chess in a mere four hours. **LARRY KAUFMAN**, grandmaster and computer expert, looks at what we know so far about AlphaZero and what implications this seemingly revolutionary step forward may have for Artificial Intelligence. And chess.

The widely publicized victory of AlphaZero against Stockfish, the strongest open-source chess engine in the world, came as a shock and not only made headlines in the chess press, but all over the world. The result is amazing enough, but before discussing the details and ramifications of this match let's look at two spectacular games from the match. In the first one (Game 10 of the ten published games) White plays a modern gambit without using an opening book, sacrifices a piece for only vague compensation, finds some brilliant quiet moves, sacrifices another pawn, and only regains the sacrificed material with interest 20 moves after the initial sacrifice! The second game also features a piece sacrifice that took more than 20 moves to recoup. How can anyone or anything play in such a risky style and not lose a single game out of a hundred against a 3400 level opponent?

AlphaZero
Stockfish 8
2017, 10th match game
Queen's Indian Defence

1.♘f3 ♘f6 2.d4 e6 3.c4 b6 4.g3 ♗b7 5.♗g2 ♗e7 6.0-0 0-0 7.d5

FROM ALPHA MALE TO ZERO

RELAX, GIVE ME SOME TIME ...

WHAT ARE YOU WRITING?

SHAKESPEARE? HAMLET?

GIVE ME FOUR MINUTES!

ALPHA ZERO

BERREND VONK

I predict an upsurge in popularity for this gambit line due to this match. While it is not new, it is quite surprising to see an engine play it without using an opening book.

7...exd5 8.♘h4 c6 9.cxd5 ♘xd5 10.♘f5 ♘c7 11.e4 d5 12.exd5 ♘xd5

12...cxd5 is more popular and probably more equal than the knight recapture.

13.♘c3 ♘xc3

13...♗f6 14.♘xd5 cxd5 15.♘e3 is normal, when White is slightly better according to both Komodo and statistics.

14.♕g4 g6 15.♘h6+!?

Any normal player (human or engine) would just recapture, 15.bxc3, with enough compensation for the pawn to claim equality.

15...♔g7 16.bxc3 ♗c8 17.♕f4 ♕d6 18.♕a4 g5

19.♖e1!!

Who wouldn't just play 19.♘g4 here, with rough equality? While the knight sacrifice played doesn't appear to win by force, it offers great practical winning chances while keeping the draw in hand (it seems). We don't know whether AlphaZero played this thinking it favoured White, or just because it thought that 19.♘g4 was a tad worse for White while the sacrifice was equal. But in any case it is a

prime example of how AlphaZero aims for the best practical chances rather than for the 'best' move. AlphaZero was designed to score points, not to provide analysis for correspondence play.

19...♔xh6 20.h4 f6 21.♗e3

21...♗f5

If 21...♔g7 22.♖ad1 ♕a3 23.♕e4 ♗c5 24.hxg5 ♗xe3 25.♖xe3 ♘c5 26.gxf6+ ♖xf6 27.♖d8 ♗e6 28.♕h4 and White is clearly better but not clearly winning.

22.♖ad1 ♛a3 23.♕c4 b5 24.hxg5+ fxg5 25.♕h4+ ♚g6

26.♕h1! ♚g7 27.♗e4 ♗g6 28.♗xg6 hxg6

29.♕h3!

It is very difficult to see that this move leads to an advantage, not just to a draw.

29...♗f6 30.♚g2 ♛xa2 31.♖h1 ♛g8

32.c4!!

The ideas are to get access to the 7th rank after 32...bxc4 33.♖b1, and to prevent a later ...♛a2 check after a rook sacrifice on e3. Another very difficult move even for an engine.

32...♖e8 33.♗d4 ♗xd4 34.♖xd4 ♖d8 35.♖xd8 ♛xd8 36.♕e6! ♘d7 37.♖d1 ♘c5 38.♖xd8 ♘xe6 39.♖xa8 ♚f6 40.cxb5 cxb5 41.♚f3 ♘d4+ 42.♚e4 ♘c6 43.♖c8 ♘e7 44.♖b8 ♘f5 45.g4 ♘h6 46.f3 ♘f7 47.♖a8 ♘d6+ 48.♚d5 ♘c4 49.♖xa7 ♘e3+ 50.♚e4 ♘c4 51.♖a6+ ♚g7 52.♖c6 ♚f7 53.♖c5 ♚e6 54.♖xg5 ♚f6 55.♖c5 g5 56.♚d4 1-0.

AlphaZero
Stockfish 8
2017, 9th match game

position after 29...♗e7

Here any strong chess player will see that 30.♗xg6 wins if the bishop is taken, but if Black first takes the knight and after 31.♕xg5 then takes the bishop on g6, it doesn't look like White has enough compensation for the piece, especially if he isn't aiming for a draw. But AlphaZero played this way and won.

30.♗xg6!! ♗xg5 31.♕xg5 fxg6 32.f5! ♖g8

Both captures on f5 lose quickly.

33.♕h6 ♕f7 34.f6

It's pretty clear that White has enough compensation for the piece to hold a draw, as it seems that Black can only 'pass' with king moves. But I imagine most GMs would agree to a draw as White here, since he is a piece down with no obvious way to play for a win. Komodo shows a zero score here at any reasonable depth.

34...♚d8 35.♚d2 ♚d7 36.♖c1 ♚d8 37.♚e3 ♚f8 38.♕c3

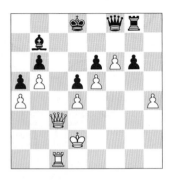

It turns out that Black cannot avoid the trade of queens. But isn't the player with an extra piece supposed to aim for a queen trade? It turns out that the resultant endings are won for White despite the piece for pawn deficit. Quite a remarkable concept if 'seen' before the initial sacrifice. My guess is that with Monte Carlo search (explained on page 34), AlphaZero was winning sometimes and drawing other times, on balance better than it could achieve without the initial sacrifice. It didn't 'know' that the sacrifice won, just that it was more likely to win than to lose, and by a bigger margin than with some quiet continuation.

38...♕b4 38...♚f7 39.♚e3 ♕d7 40.♖f1 ♕c8 41.♕xc8+ ♗xc8 42.♚f4 ♖h8 43.♚g5 ♚e8 44.♖c1 ♗d7 45.♖c7, winning. **39.♕xb4 axb4 40.♖g1 b3 41.♚c3 ♗c8 42.♚xb3 ♗d7 43.♚b4 ♗e8 44.♖a1 ♚c7 45.a5 ♗d7 46.axb6+ ♚xb6 47.♖a6+ ♚b7 48.♚c5 ♖d8 49.♖a2 ♖c8+ 50.♚d6 ♗e8 51.♚e7 g5 52.hxg5**

Now Black resigned.

Note that more than twenty moves after the initial piece sacrifice, White has not yet won material, but soon will. Although engines like Stockfish and Komodo can look ahead by forty plies (20 moves) or so in serious games, it is a selective lookahead that tends to prune sacrifices that don't pay immediate dividends. For an engine to play piece sacrifices like this (assuming they don't want to make a draw) normally requires many hours or days of analysis even on a monster machine.

Caring less about material

The DeepMind paper on the match only included ten selected games, but since there were reportedly no losses we cannot accuse them of refusing to publish their losses! The other eight games published generally showed Alpha achieving nice positional advantages and binds on Stockfish, often by sacrificing a pawn or two early on. It was relentless in exploiting these advantages. In general it seemed to care much less about material than any top level normal engine. But keep in mind that DeepMind selected the games, they are not a random sample.

According to the DeepMind paper, AlphaZero (which I'll call AZ) taught itself to play chess solely from the rules, playing thousands of games against itself to train a 'neural network' while using 'Monte Carlo Tree Search' to select moves. This would have taken years on normal personal computers, but using a vast array of thousands of 'Tensor Processing Units' custom made for the purpose it was able to reach the level of Stockfish after only four hours, and to reach the level shown in the match after nine hours. Moreover, it did the same thing (with more training time) in the Asian games 'Go' and Shogi (Japanese chess; see sidebar). Frankly this all sounds incredible and hard to believe, but I don't doubt the honesty of the team, which included at least one strong chess player (Demis Hassabis) and one chess engine author. While the match conditions were far from

The rise of AlphaZero from Go

To tell the story of AlphaZero properly requires a discussion of the Asian game called 'Go' (Wei-Chi in China, Baduk in Korea). It is perhaps the main rival to the various forms of chess among traditional two person, pure skill, mental games. It is played on a 19x19 board and typically lasts more than twice as many moves as a typical chess game, so there are more opportunities per game to go astray. Twenty years ago, while IBM's 'Deep Blue' computer was beating Kasparov in a chess match, pc Go programs were very weak. I am perhaps a 1900 Elo Go player, but back then I couldn't enjoy a game with a Go program without giving it a huge handicap. The main problem was that although one can assess a chess position reasonably well by playing out captures and counting material, pawn structure, king safety, and mobility, there is no simple way to assess a Go position. It is usually quite difficult to say which stones will live and which will die, and who will end up with more territory (the object of the game). Then someone introduced the idea of 'Monte Carlo Search', in which moves are judged by playing further moves in a random or semi-random manner and gathering statistics to choose the move. While this seems horribly inefficient, it proved to work better than previous methods. As the methods for choosing the likelihood of trying different moves improved, so did the Go engines, and by 2015 commercial Go engines had reached a level that might be compared to FM level in chess. It was widely believed that reaching Pro (similar to GM in chess) level would take another decade or so, and to defeat the World Number 1 might take two decades. Attempts to apply Monte Carlo search in chess never produced play that was even close to the level of normal chess engines. Then two years ago Google's subsidiary DeepMind announced that they had created Go playing hardware and software called 'Alpha Go' that easily defeated the European champion (probably a weak GM in chess terms) by five to zero in a match. It

combined Monte Carlo search with learning from thousands of pro games. After a few months 'training', it defeated Lee Sedol, a many-time World Champion past his prime but still in the top ten, by four to one. After another few months a new version which learned only from playing itself beat Ke Jie, the current World number 1, by three to zero. Finally, AlphaZero, which taught itself using only the rules of the game, defeated the previous version by 60 to 40. All of this was incredible, although how much was due to the programming and how much to the custom-made very expensive hardware is not clear. But it should be mentioned that shortly after the Ke Jie match, a free PC engine ('Leela') appeared with similar ideas and reached at least what we would call IM level in chess on a normal pc. Recently there are reports that private versions of two other programs using these ideas have surpassed the level of Ke Jie.

It was obvious that DeepMind would try these ideas with chess, especially since they have a chess master (Demis Hassabis, FIDE 2249) and an author of a 'learning' chess engine called 'Giraffe' on the team. But the strength of the top 3 chess engines is so high (3400 or so Elo, roughly a thousand Elo above 'Giraffe') that it seemed improbable that a learning and/or Monte Carlo machine could reach this level soon. Yet DeepMind managed to create a machine this way that crushed Stockfish by 28 to zero with 72 draws. To prove their point further, they did the same for the Japanese version of chess ('Shogi'), which crushed the top pc engine 'Elmo' (which had defeated the human champ two to zero) by 90 to 8 with 2 draws. DeepMind has demonstrated that a machine can teach itself to play pure skill games with clearly defined goals and rules far better than any human can play them, but whether this can apply to other things where goals and rules are not so clear remains to be seen. There is little doubt though that the day when computers surpass humans at all mental tasks is closer than it seemed before this development, though it may still be far away.

fair (see sidebar), the result was so one-sided and some of the games so amazing that it's hard to deny Alpha's superiority.

The hardware

While there's still a lot we don't know about AZ, I think there are three factors that made it so strong at all three games. The training by self-play method is obviously very efficient, and the DeepMind team would like to attribute most of the achievement to this, I think. But the hardware used, both for the training and the actual match, played a huge role, and this cannot be duplicated by others without spending a lot of money. The point is that the hardware is fundamentally different from the hardware used to run normal chess engines like Stockfish; Stockfish would not benefit from the DeepMind hardware, while AZ would be crippled on the type of machine Stockfish ran on.

The third factor is a bit harder to explain. AZ uses Monte Carlo Tree Search (MCTS) while normal chess engines use 'MiniMax' and 'Alpha-Beta'. MCTS expands the tree probabilistically; for example at a given node it might assign a 50% chance of selecting a capture check but only a 0.1% chance of selecting an unprovoked knight retreat. MCTS has been used very successfully for Go playing engines for many years now, but no one ever wrote a strong chess engine using MCTS. It was considered unsuitable for chess, and indeed it may be unsuitable for chess on an everyday dual-core laptop, but DeepMind has shown that with the right hardware (and programming) it works well for chess. What they have not yet shown, in my opinion, is that the neural network training works as well as a chess-knowledge based MCTS engine on the hardware they used for AZ. Since the cost of renting hardware sufficient to duplicate the DeepMind training is probably too high to recover by software sales, we might not find out the answer to this

crucial question any time soon, but we might be surprised.

The use of MCTS explains a lot about the style of play of AZ. It will be reluctant to try sacrifices initially, but once it does try a sacrifice, if it scores well it will keep playing it. In that way it is much more like a human player than is a conventional chess engine. Basically, it will play whatever works without prejudice. This leads to much more exciting play than is typical of engines, and to a focus on practical chances rather than finding the 'best' move, which often doesn't exist, if several moves lead to a win or to a draw when there is no win. But I should point out that normal engines can be made to play many of the shocking AZ moves by appropriate settings. For example, Komodo (of which I'm co-author with Mark Lefler) can be given a huge 'Dynamism' setting and it will play seemingly in AZ style, but against equal opposition it will lose many games if set this way.

PSYCHOLOGICAL WARFARE IS THE ONLY WAY LEFT TO WIN

WHAT ARE YOU STARING AT?

What is AZ's rating?

How strong is AZ in chess? First we must determine the Elo level of its sole opponent, Stockfish 8. According to engine rating lists such as CCRL, Stockfish, Komodo, and Houdini are all rated around 3400 running on a 4 core machine. These ratings are probably a bit inflated for several reasons, but since Stockfish ran on (at least) a 32 core machine for this match, the 3400 figure is reasonable for it. As further evidence, Komodo (playing on a 24 core machine) has played many matches (at 45' + 15") against grandmasters giving odds of f7-pawn, rook for knight, and two pawns (various), without losing a single game after its very first match (at c2 + f2 odds), with about half the games drawn and half won by Komodo. Based on estimates of the Elo value of these handicaps from Komodo selfplay, the overall performance rating of Komodo was in the ballpark of 3400, so this seems like a fair figure to use. Simple math would put AZ at 3500. But this leads to talking about the meaning of 3000+ ratings, and the limit that would be achieved by perfect play.

As ratings approach and exceed 3000, the effects of draws and colours grow. Top players like to think that they can draw at will with White against anyone, and while this is clearly not literally true, it is very hard to beat 2800+ humans if they aim to draw as White. Perhaps above some level (3200? 3400?) it becomes literally true. Note that in this match Stockfish drew 47 out of 50 with White (losing the other 3), without even being told that it was playing a superior opponent, and without a book. If the weaker player can always draw with White, then he can always score at least 25% in a match, which would limit the rating of any opponent (even perfect play) to under 3600 (using 3400 as the 'unbeatable with White' figure). However, an opponent who wins 28 out of 50 with White and draws all 50 with Black (producing the same 64 to 36 score as in this match) would get a 3500 rating. Then if another opponent did the same to him he would get 3600, and the next 3700, with no clear obvious limit. The rating system just breaks down at these levels because it ignores colours and it rates draws. Even if we solve the colour problem (for example by rating two game matches only, one with each colour, as a single game), the increasing frequency of draws at higher levels would limit the maximum rating, perhaps to somewhere around 4000. The problem is that White's advantage in chess, though substantial (as this match showed dramatically, White winning by 25 to 3 in decisive games), is generally believed to be far from enough to win. My own engine tests suggest that if White starts with two moves instead of one, he still isn't winning, but with three he is. If White started with enough advantage to be right on the win/draw edge, then the draw percentage would remain

Was it a fair match?

Was the match with Stockfish a valid test of which is the stronger chess player? No, but I doubt that a fair match would have changed the winner.
Let's see how the conditions favoured AlphaZero.

❶ 'Hash size' (a measure for short-term storage) for Stockfish was set very low (at 1 GB). This probably cost about 20 Elo.

❷ Stockfish cannot make much use of more than 32 threads, but it reportedly ran on 64 on a machine with only 32 cores. This nearly halved the speed. Maybe another 20 Elo.

❸ Stockfish used its last official release, Stockfish 8, whereas the latest development version was perhaps another 20 Elo or so stronger under the match conditions. Here I agree with DeepMind's decision, as if they had used a development version some would have called it buggy.

❹ No opening books. This favoured AlphaZero as it was tuned from the opening position while Stockfish is tuned from book positions. Also it led to minimal variety in the openings, which meant that favourable openings were often repeated with similar results. This one is hard to quantify.

❺ Fixed time (one minute) per move. This meant that all of Stockfish's time usage algorithms were wasted; maybe another 20 Elo. In AlphaZero's defence, they would argue that they hadn't bothered with time management, so using real time controls would have favoured Stockfish.

❻ Hardware. AlphaZero ran on much more expensive, custom hardware. However Stockfish would not have benefited from their hardware. AlphaZero used processors that excel at 'floating point' math, which

Stockfish does not require. Stockfish ran on almost the best hardware it could benefit from as currently written. My best guess is that the Stockfish hardware probably could be purchased for around $10,000, while the AlphaZero hardware would probably cost many times that. Whether this is fair is a matter of opinion. Defenders of AlphaZero may point out that Stockfish looked at more than a thousand times as many positions per second as did AlphaZero, but there isn't much difference between looking at 1000 positions and throwing out 999 of them, or doing some intelligent analysis to decide which one of the 1000 deserves serious consideration.

'Probably Stockfish was handicapped by about the 100 Elo by which it lost the match.'

As for the choice of Stockfish as the opponent, I don't think it would have been much different with either Komodo or Houdini. All three engines are rated very close at non-blitz levels, and each won one of the latest TCEC championships (standard, rapid, and blitz). Although the engines are significantly different from each other, the differences are tiny when compared to the difference between any of them and AlphaZero.

So probably Stockfish was handicapped by about the 100 Elo by which it lost the match. Would it have been a tossup under optimal (for Stockfish) conditions? Probably not, because the 64 to 36 score is misleading. The 28 to zero score excluding draws suggests a much larger real gap in strength. My best guess is that with ideal conditions Stockfish would still have lost by something like 15 to 5 with 80 draws.

around 50% regardless of how high the level of the players reached, until they approached perfect play. But this would require some rule change that favoured White, for example 'neither player can castle on the same side as the opponent has castled'. Or we can give each player a fixed amount of time (plus some small increment or delay) with all draws to be replayed using the remaining time until someone wins (this is done in Shogi, where draws are rare). Doing this, or simply just rating decisive games, would allow for an almost unlimited Elo ceiling. Already in Go (which has almost zero draws) AZ is at least 2000 Elo above the human champ, and we would see the same thing in chess if draws were not rated. If this were done, AZ would have an infinite performance rating so far in chess, perhaps 5000 or more once it eventually loses a game!

And now what?

So what does the AZ performance mean for the future of chess? In the short term, that depends on Google's plans for it. If they wanted to make a commercial version to sell (or even give away) it would have a huge impact, in my opinion. It's not just the extra Elo points over current software. You will often hear top players say things like 'the engine can't be trusted in closed positions, or certain endgames' or 'move x is better according to the engine, but move y is a better choice for a human because the following moves are more natural and/or easier to find' or 'the engine shows a big score for White but shows no way to make progress in the principal variation'. I think these claims are currently valid, but if a MCTS engine (like AZ) becomes available that is at least as strong as the top 3 engines, they won't generally be true anymore. MCTS automatically corrects these problems (imperfectly, it's true) at the cost of risking missing long forced tactical lines. But it seems from the AZ result that this is much

less of a problem than we all thought it would be. Maybe if you get good enough positions, any long tactical sequences would be wins for you, so if you miss them you still go undefeated. At least that's what it looks like to me.

Most likely though, Google will not release the engine, although I could imagine that they might make it available online for use. So then the question is whether others will be able to duplicate Google's feat. It seems that a total duplication is unlikely for a few years because the hardware needed for the training of the neural network is too costly to duplicate. But perhaps semi-affordable hardware could duplicate the feat in a few months or less. Moreover it's not clear whether the Neural Network and self-play is the best way; it seems likely to me that some information other than just the rules would speed up the process. I'll predict that within a year we will see some MCTS engine (with or without Neural Network self-play) that will be stronger than normal engines on hardware that costs under $5,000 (maybe way under). If so, everyone will switch to it, because it will play much more like a super-human and will recommend opening moves that are much harder to meet in practice. We may also see that the engine choices become much harder to criticize.

My biggest hope for the future of chess is that normal chess games will be replaced by two-game matches (either simultaneous or with a total time allocation for the two games)

> '**I can easily imagine that a solution to global warming might be found by some future AZ, or a solution to many of the diseases of aging, since at least the goals of these "games" are clear, if not the rules.'**

with the openings to be chosen by chance from some predetermined set, with each player getting to play the White side of the same opening once. This is already the way computer chess rating lists and the top 'TCEC' engine tournament are run, as well as most 8x8 checkers tournaments. Kramnik has proposed such balloted openings. It would favour the stronger players (Carlsen should love it!), reduce draws, and eliminate preparation for specific opponents. No more Berlin Walls game after game! I think that when strong MCTS engines become available something like this will catch on, as traditional chess will be more and more a memory and preparation contest.

Beyond chess

What are the consequences for the world outside of chess, Go, and shogi? It's not yet clear that the AZ approach will apply to endeavours that don't have clearly defined rules and goals. I don't think it will lead to an immediate cure for cancer, for example. The goal is clear enough, but the rules are quite vague. But I think it does mean that application to medicine and solving many other of the world's big problems may not be as far in the future as we had thought. I can easily imagine, for example, that a solution to global warming might be found by some future AZ, or a solution to many of the diseases of aging, since at least the goals of these 'games' are clear, if not the rules. I'm 70 years old, and my prospects of living with decent health to 100, 110, or even 120 are not as far-fetched as they seemed a few months ago. But I'm not betting on it yet. ∎

OLE KRISTIAN STRØM

The Tiger of Madras bites back

Vishy Anand Rapid World Champion without a single loss

No one would have blamed Vishy Anand had he stayed at home after his bottom place at the London Classic. He might have done so, had not his wife emphatically advised him to travel to the Rapid & Blitz World Championships in Riyadh anyway. Great foresight and insight! A fortnight after his 48th birthday, Anand sparkled and won the rapid world title. **ADHIBAN BASKARAN** watched his legendary countryman in admiration and reveals that he also contributed to his success. Maybe.

Rapid World Champion Vishy Anand is visibly delighted with his wonderful performance.

At the end of November I came to know about the possibility of the World Rapid & Blitz Championship to be held in Saudi Arabia. I had mixed feelings about the place, but at the same time I was happy to visit this country which so far had stayed off my radar for both chess events and for tourism! While many decided to use social media to criticize the choice of country for such an event, I wanted to give them a chance before I made up my mind.

Hopefully next year players from Iran and Israel will get visas, too, as I was pleasantly surprised by the amount of effort put in by the organizers to ensure an excellently run event.

On the first day I had the privilege of sitting next to Vishy Anand on the bus that took us from our hotel to the opening ceremony. It was a long ride and I used the opportunity to ask Vishy: 'Can you give me some tips on how to play awesome and also be consistent at the same time?' To which he mockingly replied: 'Consistency? Did you see my recent rapid event? (He meant the Rapid &Blitz in St. Louis) I was placed last!'

Hoping to cheer him up I ventured: 'But in the World Rapid & Blitz you are consistent, right?' To which he replied again: 'Well, last time wasn't great either!'

I realized that I had provoked him unintentionally and I hurriedly changed the topic. But the damage had already been done. I suppose Anand thought to himself: 'It is time I put an end to these retirement rumours and show the world (and this idiot sitting next to me ☺) what I am capable of!'

Unbeaten
That's the unofficial version of why Anand won the Rapid world title, staying unbeaten for 15 rounds! (And mind you, in the ensuing Blitz,

where he finished third, he only lost one game from 21, against Nepomniachtchi, due to a hallucination.) The official version has it that his wife Aruna insisted that Vishy play and urged him to skip a couple of days of family vacation, which he later joined as the Rapid World Champion!

But before we look at Vishy's best efforts, let's have a look at the game that Magnus Carlsen played in the very first round. Against the opponent that knocked him out of the World Cup. I wonder what his secret is!

Magnus Carlsen
Bu Xiangzhi
Riyadh rapid 15' 10" 2017 (1)

position after 26.♕e2

26...♘h4 So far things had been

going decently for the World Champion, but from here on he is outplayed by his Chinese nightmare! **27.♘xh4 gxh4 28.♕h5 ♖g8 29.♗f1 ♖dg7 30.♔h1 ♕e7** 30...g5 was a better move order, with advantage to Black. **31.♕f3** 31.♗xe5 f3 looks scary for White, but he can hold after 32.g4! hxg3 33.♗xg3 ♖xg3 34.fxg3 ♖xg3 with sufficient compensation for the exchange. **31...♖g5 32.a4 ♗f7 33.♖d7 ♕e6 34.♕e2** Clearly better was 34.♕a3!, followed by f3, and White is doing great. **34...♗h5 35.f3 ♖g3 36.♔h2 ♕b6!**

A stunning move, preparing the nasty ...♗xf3 or ...♖xh3+.
37.c5 ♕xc5 38.♔h1 And Carlsen resigned before Bu could play 38...♖xh3+ 39.gxh3 ♕g1 mate.

Anand had a better start. One of his finest games he played in Round 2.

NOTES BY
Adhiban Baskaran

Vishy Anand
Peter Leko
Riyadh rapid 15' 10" 2017 (2)
Giuoco Piano

1.e4 e5 2.♘f3 ♘c6 3.♗c4
This is the only refutation of the Berlin Defence!

S. P. Sethuraman and our reporter Adhiban Baskaran ('A proud moment to be an Indian') clearly appreciate Vishy Anand's humour.

16...c5!? offered more chances to equalize, but White is able to retain a pull after 17.♗xf4! ♘xf4 18.♕d2 ♘g6 19.♖ad1, with pressure on the centre. **17.e5** After this Vishy never gave the ever-solid Leko a chance.
17...c5

18.♗xg6! One of the key differences between the elite and the rest is the ability to assess the correct exchange operations.
18...♘xg6 19.♗g5 ♘e7
19...♕b6 20.♘h5, with a brutal attack on the dark squares.
20.♕d2 The beginning of the end...
20...h6

21.♗f6! ♔h7 22.♘g5+! ♔g8 23.♘h5 Anand's forces make a deadly attacking combination (not to mention that the a1-rook can always be involved in the attack with ♖a3!). More colourful was 23.e6! fxe6 24.♘h5! gxf6 25.♘xe6 ♗xe6 26.♖xe6!, with a winning attack. It is not an easy move to see, because ♕h6 might be the one you want to make! But 26.♕xh6 ♘f5 27.♕g6+ ♔f8 28.g4 ♗f7 29.♕xf5 ♗xh5 30.gxh5 is only sufficient for a draw.
23...gxf6

3...♗c5 4.0-0 ♘f6 5.d3 0-0 6.h3 d6 7.c3 a6 8.a4 ♗a7 9.♘bd2 9...♘e7 10.♖e1 c6

11.♗b3 A logical deviation from the game Karjakin-Leko from the World Blitz 2016 that saw 11.b4 ♘g6 12.d4 exd4 13.cxd4 d5 14.exd5 ♘xd5 15.♕b3 ♗e6 16.b5 axb5 17.axb5 ♘df4 18.♗xe6 ♘xe6 19.♗a3 ♘xd4 20.♘xd4 ♗xd4 21.♖ad1 ♖e8 22.♘e4 ♕b6 23.♘d6 ♖xe1+ 24.♖xe1 ♗xf2+ 25.♔h1 ♗xe1 (25...♕c7, and Black is just better) 26.♕xf7+ ♔h8 27.♗b2, and White won (27.♘e8 was what Leko was expecting, after which he had intended to play 27...♗c3).
11...♘g6 12.♗c2!? A nice novelty; now Black will struggle to equalize.
12...♖e8 13.d4

13...♘h5 After 13...h6, 14.a5!? fixes the pawn structure favourably: 14...♗e6 15.♘f1, with a better position for White. **14.♘f1 ♘hf4 15.♘g3** White has achieved a slightly better position, which is quite an achievement by modern standards ☺. **15...exd4 16.cxd4**

16...d5

24.♘xf7! ♚xf7 25.♕xh6 ♘f5 26.♕h7+ ♚f8 27.exf6 ♗e6 28.♘f4 ♕xf6 29.♘g6+ ♕xg6 30.♕xg6

A great calculation feat to see all the way to this material imbalance. Black's forces are unable to put up a

fight against the mighty combination of the queen and the pawns.
30...♘g7 31.♖e3
I would have preferred to include the only sleepy piece in White's camp with 31.♖a3!.
31...♖e7 32.♖ae1
And Vishy converted confidently:
32...♖ae8 33.♕g3

33...♖f7
As 33...cxd4 allows 34.♖xe6, winning.
34.h4 ♗b8 35.♖ge3 ♖fe7 36.dxc5 ♗f7 37.♕f6 ♖xe3 38.♖xe3 ♖xe3 39.fxe3 ♗c7 40.g4 ♘e8 41.♕h8+ ♗g8 42.h5 ♗d8 43.♕h6+ ♘g7 44.♕d6+ ♗e7 45.♕b8+ ♘e8 46.b4 a5 47.♕xb7 axb4 48.♕xb4 ♘f6

49.♕f4 ♚e8 50.c6 ♗e6 51.h6

There are just way too many pawns... Black resigned.

And here are some further samples of the ease and pleasure Vishy was playing with.

Vishy Anand
Anton Demchenko
Riyadh rapid 15' 10" 2017 (4)

position after 24...♗f8

Black has just played 24...♗f8 and Anand finishes off the game in style.
25.♘h5 ♚e7 26.♕g4! Preparing the nasty 27.♘xf6.

26...♗h6 26...♖h6 is met by 27.♗xf7! ♚xf7 28.♕g8+ ♚e7

MARIA EMELIANOVA

29.♖g7+, with a winning advantage. Black's only option was 26...♕d4!? 27.♘xf6 ♖xc4, getting rid of White's major attacking powers: 28.♘xc4 ♕xc4. Now White is unable to finish the game off and has to be content with 29.b3 ♕d4 30.♖d1 ♕a7 31.♕g5 ♗c6 and although Black's position looks dangerous, he may be holding on...

27.♘xf6! ♗xd2 28.♘d5+ ♔e8

29.♕g8+ A pretty finish! 1-0.

Luke McShane
Vishy Anand
Riyadh rapid 15' 10'' 2017 (7)

position after 50.♕f4

While watching the game I saw the only remaining trick and was happy to see Vishy play it: **50...♕e6!** Creating a threat...

51.♕f3 And Luke McShane noticed it too late...

51...♕h3+!! 52.♔xh3 ♖h1
Mate. Now that's just so pretty!

Tricky, solid and objective was the mix that worked perfectly for Vishy. Of great importance was his win in the penultimate round against Alexander Grischuk.

NOTES BY
Adhiban Baskaran

Vishy Anand
Alexander Grischuk
Riyadh rapid 15' 10'' 2017 (1)
Ruy Lopez, Berlin Defence

1.e4 e5 2.♘f3 ♘c6 3.♗b5 ♘f6 4.d3 ♗c5 5.♘bd2 d6 6.c3 0-0 7.0-0

7...a6
Maybe Grischuk was hoping that this would be sufficient to save the day? More solid was 7...♘e7 8.d4 exd4 9.cxd4 ♗b6 10.♖e1 ♗g4 11.h3 ♗h5 12.a4!?, as was seen in Anand-Topalov, Moscow Candidates 2016.

8.♗xc6!?
Vishy doesn't need another invitation! After all he is a knight's person, whereas Fischer and Kasparov preferred bishops!

8...bxc6 9.d4 exd4 10.cxd4 ♗b6 11.♕c2

11...c5
11...♖e8! was the right move order, so I assume Grischuk forgot the move order subtleties: 12.♖e1 c5 13.d5 ♗g4

Riyadh 2017 rapid

1	Vishy Anand	IND	2758	11	2874
2	Vladimir Fedoseev	RUS	2771	11	2871
3	Ian Nepomniachtchi	RUS	2780	11	2843
4	Bu Xiangzhi	CHN	2654	10	2867
5	Magnus Carlsen	NOR	2908	10	2823
6	Alexander Grischuk	RUS	2813	10	2827
7	Boris Savchenko	RUS	2685	10	2786
8	Rauf Mamedov	AZE	2695	10	2753
9	Gadir Guseinov	AZE	2714	10	2754
10	Peter Svidler	RUS	2743	9½	2805
11	Wang Hao	CHN	2770	9½	2814
12	Yu Yangyi	CHN	2752	9½	2778
13	Vladislav Artemiev	RUS	2687	9½	2754
14	Vladimir Onischuk	UKR	2748	9½	2757
15	Ding Liren	CHN	2734	9½	2748
16	Pentala Harikrishna	IND	2687	9½	2737
17	Sergey Grigoriants	RUS	2572	9½	2659
18	Zhao Jun	CHN	2600	9½	2618
19	Levan Pantsulaia	GEO	2654	9	2806
20	Ivan Saric	CRO	2597	9	2716
21	Aleksandr Rakhmanov	RUS	2649	9	2728
22	Evgeny Alekseev	RUS	2681	9	2730
23	Shakhriyar Mamedyarov	AZE	2814	9	2747
24	Eltaj Safarli	AZE	2694	9	2725
25	Jan-Krzysztof Duda	POL	2678	9	2698
26	Wang Yue	CHN	2702	9	2721
27	Dmitry Kokarev	RUS	2668	9	2678
28	Anton Korobov	UKR	2765	9	2708
29	Levon Aronian	ARM	2819	9	2706
30	Le Quang Liem	VIE	2750	9	2686
31	Sergei Zhigalko	BLR	2707	9	2686
32	Varuzhan Akobian	USA	2620	9	2647
33	David Anton	ESP	2732	9	2638
34	Sergey Karjakin	RUS	2757	9	2653
35	Alexey Dreev	RUS	2659	8½	2699
36	Martyn Kravtsiv	UKR	2610	8½	2760
37	Rustam Kasimdzhanov	UZB	2679	8½	2721
38	Ivan Cheparinov	FID	2694	8½	2701
39	Richard Rapport	HUN	2748	8½	2691
40	Sanan Sjugirov	RUS	2729	8½	2662
41	Maxime Vachier-Lagrave	FRA	2839	8½	2650
42	Hrant Melkumyan	ARM	2696	8½	2625
43	Nguyen Ngoc Truong Son	VIE	2693	8½	2611
44	Baadur Jobava	GEO	2672	8	2675
45	Laurent Fressinet	FRA	2612	8	2745
46	Viktor Laznicka	CZE	2640	8	2773
47	Giga Quparadze	GEO	2614	8	2686
48	Pavel Ponkratov	RUS	2673	8	2694
49	Alexander Moiseenko	UKR	2618	8	2705
50	Peter Leko	HUN	2671	8	2677
51	Gabriel Sargissian	ARM	2673	8	2664
52	Anton Demchenko	RUS	2667	8	2646
53	Zoltan Almasi	HUN	2638	8	2647
54	David Howell	ENG	2626	8	2645

134 players, 15 rounds

14.b3 ♗a5!. This is the point. In the game, Anand was able to delay ♖e1 until the situation favoured him. 15.♖e3 ♗xf3! (knights are more important in this line ☺) 16.♘xf3 ♕e7, and this was fine for Black in Bogdanovich-Le Quang Liem, Ho Chi Minh City 2017.

12.d5

From here on in, Vishy makes it look so easy and his pieces have an amazing flow to them.

12...♖e8 13.b3

13...♗g4 After this White is practically unstoppable!

Black's last chance was 13...a5!? 14.a4 (14.♗b2 a4, and Black is completely fine) 14...c6! 15.dxc6 d5 16.exd5 (16.e5 ♘g4, and White has to be careful not to end up worse) 16...♘xd5 17.♗b2 ♕xc6, and the bishops will compensate for the wrecked pawn structure.

14.♗b2 ♗h5

15.♖ae1!
Full focus on the kingside.
15...♗g6 16.♗xf6!
What did I say? Yet again Vishy decides to get rid of the knight, leaving Black with practically hopeless bishops!

16...♕xf6 17.♘c4 ♗a7 18.♕d3 h6 19.♖e3 ♖ad8 20.g3 ♗h7 21.♖fe1 g5 22.♕e2 ♔g7 23.♖d1 ♕g6 24.♖e1 ♕f6 25.♔g2 g4 26.♘h4 ♕g5

27.f4!
After optimally improving his pieces and killing any possible counterplay attempts, Anand proceeds to the next phase...
27...gxf3+ 28.♕xf3 ♕f6 29.♕e2 ♕g5 30.♖f1 ♔g8 31.♘f5
The a7-bishop remains a sad spectator.
31...♖xe4 32.♘xh6+ ♕xh6 33.♖xe4 ♗xe4+ 34.♕xe4 ♔f8 35.♖e1 ♕f6 36.♖e2 ♗b6 37.h4 ♔g7 38.♖f2 ♕g6 39.♖f5 ♔f8 40.h5 ♕h7 41.g4 ♖e8 42.♕f3 ♔g8

43.♔h3!
Even Karpov would be proud of Vishy's play. See Karpov-Kasparov, Moscow World Championship match 1985, Game 4, 1-0. This game is very similar to that famous opposite-coloured bishop middlegame in which Karpov placed all his forces on the light squares!
43...♖e1 44.♕f4 ♔f8 45.♕g5

♕h8 46.♖f3 ♕g7 47.♕xg7+ ♔xg7 48.g5 ♖d1 49.♘e3 ♖h1+ 50.♔g4 c4

Finally the bishop breaks free, but unfortunately it is too little too late ☺.

51.♘f5+ ♔f8 52.bxc4 ♖g1+ 53.♖g3 ♖c1 54.g6 fxg6 55.hxg6 ♖xc4+ 56.♔h5 ♗d4 57.♖g4

Black resigned. Even in the final position, all White's forces are on light squares, spelling pure agony for the sad dark-squared bishop!

After 15 rounds three players topped the standings: Anand, Fedoseev and Nepomniachtchi. But only the first two in the tiebreaks would fight for the highest honour! Suddenly it was a two-game blitz match (3' 2") between Anand and Fedoseev that would decide the winner! Vishy once again showed his superiority and won convincingly, hinting that he was already ready for next day's blitz event ☺. But kudos to Fedoseev for putting up an inspiring performance! 'Nepo' finished 3rd and as usual remained with the same poker expression as always, so I wasn't sure whether he was happy with his

performance or not ☺. When they announced Vishy Anand as the winner of the World Rapid Championship and played the national anthem of India, it was a proud moment to be an Indian! Personally I swore an oath to make it happen again!

Vishy thanked everyone, saying: 'It is nice to have people rooting for you... But you need to give them something to root for!' He mentioned the games he was most pleased with and described the following win, which we bring with his own comments, as 'especially sweet'.

NOTES BY
Vishy Anand

Magnus Carlsen
Vishy Anand
Riyadh rapid 15' 10" 2017 (9)
Nimzo-Indian Defence,
Rubinstein Variation

1.d4 ♘f6 2.c4 e6 3.♘c3 ♗b4 4.e3 0-0 5.♗d3 d5 6.a3 ♗xc3+ 7.bxc3 dxc4 8.♗xc4 c5 9.♘f3 ♕c7 10.♗e2 b6 11.♗b2

Thus far, Carlsen has been following his game against Ding Liren at the 2017 Champions Showdown in St. Louis, where he was Black and now played 11...♗a6.

11...♗b7 12.0-0 ♘bd7 13.c4 ♖ac8

13...♘g4 is premature, as 14.d5 exd5 15.cxd5 ♘gf6 16.d6 is unpleasant for Black.

14.♖c1 ♖fd8 15.♕b3 ♘g4 16.g3

After 16.d5 exd5 17.cxd5 ♘df6 favours Black. **16...♘gf6**

It is useful to have the long diagonal open. This turned out to be very important!

17.♖fd1 ♘e4 18.♘e1

18...♘d6? Having provoked g3, I could just have played 18...♘df6!, as after 19.f3 ♘xg3 20.hxg3 ♕xg3+ 21.♔f1 ♘h5! is winning. **19.d5 exd5 20.cxd5** Still, I felt that his centre would need time to get rolling.

20...c4 21.♕c2 b5 Now I am ready to counter with ...♘c5.

22.♘g2 After 22.e4 ♖e8 23.f3 f5 24.exf5 ♘xf5 (or 24...♘b6) Black is much better.

'It is nice to have people rooting for you… But you need to give them something to root for!' Anand described his win against Carlsen as 'especially sweet'.

22…♘c5 23.♘f4 ♕e7 24.♗g4
Now the game gets very sharp.

24…♖c7 25.♕c3 25.♖e1 ♘de4!
(25…♗c8 26.♗xc8 ♖cxc8 allows
27.e4!) 26.f3 ♘f6 is fine for Black.
25…f5 Black's king has been
weakened, but at least I get the
e4-square. After 25…f6 26.♗e6+
♔h8 27.♕c2 ♗c8 28.♗c3 White has
an edge. **26.♗f3**

26…♖cd7
Instead, 26…♘de4 27.♕b4 a6 28.h4
wasn't very clear. I still wasn't sure
where the d6-knight belonged.
27.♕b4 ♘b3 28.♘e6
Better was 28.♖c2 a5 29.♕e1 ♘e4,
with an equal position.
28…♘xc1 29.♖xc1

29…♘c8
The move I was happy to have seen
in advance.
After 29…a5 the comp points this
one out: 30.♕e1 (30.♕xa5 runs into
30…♖a8) 30…♘e4 31.♗xe4 fxe4
32.♘xd8 ♕xd8 33.a4 ♖xd5, and this
is about equal, since the dark-squared
bishop gives enough compensation
for the pawn.
**30.♕xb5 ♖xd5 31.♗xd5 ♖xd5
32.♕b4 ♘d6**
Black has nothing better.

33.♘c5?
At this point, we both felt that this
would lead to a draw. Since I had
four minutes left, I was able to spend
some time looking for more. After
about two minutes I suddenly saw the
winning line.
White should have played 33.♘f4!,
when after 33…♕e4 34.♘xd5 ♕xd5!
35.♔f1 c3! (35…♕h1+? 36.♔e2 or
35…♕d3+? 36.♔e1 ♗f3 37.♕d2, both
winning) 36.♕xc3 ♕h1+ 37.♔e2
♕f3+ 38.♔e1 ♕h1+ 39.♔d2 ♘e4+
the game should end in a draw. And
after 33…♕b5 34.♕c3 ♖b3 35.♕d4 h6
36.h4 ♔h7 it also seems that neither
side will really be able to improve.
33…♖xc5 34.♕xc5 ♕e4

White resigned in view of 35.♔f1 and
now:
– 35…♕d3+ 36.♔g1 (36.♔e1 ♗f3 –
if the queen had been on b4 here, it
would have been able to come to
d2, but on c5 the queen is helpless)
36…♕e4 was what we had both seen
originally.
– 35…♕h1+! 36.♔e2 ♗f3+ (the point)
37.♔d2 ♘e4+ wins a piece.
A hugely important victory, both for
my morale and for my score. ∎

SAUDI ARABIAN KNIGHTS

It is an elementary precept of business negotiation to insert all important clauses into a contract before signing. Alas, with the dysfunctional governing body of our noble game, pecuniary priorities invariably trump points of principle. It therefore came as no surprise that FIDE failed to ensure that all qualifiers for the King Salman World Rapid and Blitz Championships in Riyadh, Saudi Arabia, received visas. The omission to safeguard all its members from discriminatory political treatment was a dereliction of duty – a further addition to the bulging catalogue of breaches of FIDE's own statutes, and those of the IOC, from which we collectively crave recognition. Given the fraught situation in the Gulf region, it was obvious all along that the participation of representatives of Qatar, Iran and the unmentionable Zionist enemy Israel would prove problematic.

Given the ethical uncertainties, why then did your scribe – a trenchant critic of the current maladministration – scurry to become the first entrant in the tournament – thereby handing FIDE an unexpected propaganda coup? Undoubtedly the massive $2 million prize-fund played a part in my decision, although I never considered it likely that I would be capable of competing for the very highest prizes. The opportunity to visit an important country – one that until as recently as 2016 fell outside the FIDE ambit – was perhaps a greater draw. But essentially, any potential scruples were swiftly assuaged by the firm conviction that chess players should never be placed in the position where they have to choose between making a moral stand and furthering their career. Besides, my mischievous nature wanted to see how the FIDE Vice Presidents from Israel, Iran and Qatar would react to seeing their own players getting well and truly shafted.

Even the most casual observer will have noticed that the Wahhabist kingdom is undergoing wrenching changes. Hitherto unassailable princes have been detained (albeit in pampered luxury) in a huge crackdown on corruption. From 2018 women will be allowed to drive and movie theatres open. Whether these reforms will continue, or where it will all lead, is anyone's guess. But when Malcolm Pein, at a meeting at London's famous Dorchester Hotel, suggested to the high Saudi officials that they would score a notable public relations victory, in contradistinction to their despised rivals Iran, by allowing female competitors to dispense with the reviled hijab, it fell on receptive ears.

The issue of visas, however, proved intractable. If any 'problem' country was going to receive them it was clearly going to be fellow Sunni-Arab Qatar, and they got them only at the last moment – theoretically in time for both events, but practically only for the blitz. I twice asked Grandmaster Mohammed Al-Modiahki – a vociferous Twitter-censurer of the shabby treatment that had been meted out to Qataris – what representations FIDE Vice President Khalifa al-Hitmi had made on their behalf, but was met with telling silence. At least both he and his wife, Zhu Chen, got to Riyadh in the end.

Only one Iranian was qualified – Sarasadat Khademalsharieh – the 4th placed finisher in the previous year's Women's Rapid. She reluctantly withdrew, on Foreign Office advice, back in November, but that did not prevent FIDE from falsely claiming, one month later, that she had been granted a visa, which she most certainly had

> **'Besides, my mischievous nature wanted to see how the FIDE Vice Presidents from Israel, Iran and Qatar would react to seeing their own players getting well and truly shafted.'**

not. Sara's lack of support from her own federation leaves the distinct impression that the political advancement of President Mehrdad Pahlevanzadeh and FIDE Vice President Mohammad Kambouzia are considered of greater importance than the chess aspirations of a mere girl. It may be difficult to maintain such an attitude of misogynistic dismissiveness, though, for the next two World Rapid and Blitz Championships, which are also slated for Saudi Arabia. By then it is possible, or even probable, that she will be joined as a qualifier by some of the numerous young male talents. Pressure to participate may prove irresistible – particularly if favoured son, Ehsan Ghaem Maghami, also fancies a go.

STORIES

Predictably though, it was the Israelis who got stiffed again. The Association of Chess Professionals President, Emil Sutovsky, was his ever-voluble self, misdirecting his spleen towards the participants, rather than the officials who make the decisions. I asked him what Israel Gelfer – a man who notoriously launched a discreditable career within FIDE by failing to stand up for Israeli interests at the Dubai Olympiad 1986, and actively working against them, by disingenuously testifying against fellow countryman Vadim Milov over Libya in 2004 – had done on their behalf? 'He is not our representative in FIDE', came the snooty reply. Wrong, Emil. He may no longer occupy the post of Delegate, but he is a Vice President, which is far more important. In fairness, Gelfer did speak up on this occasion, although how much of this is exculpatory posturing, because of his own greatly weakened position within the Israeli Federation, is open to debate.

Politics aside, the King Salman R&B Championships were actually very well organised – particularly so given the exceedingly short time-frame. From the surfeit of friendly staff who greeted us at the airport, to the specially painted buses, to the comfortable hotels with delicious food (albeit without accompanying alcoholic libations), to the excellent venue with refreshments, live traditional music and photogenic falcon – all was well. It was genuinely a pleasure to be there. Inevitably there was the odd glitch – particularly when exhausted participants were escorted home only at 1 a.m. after the grand gala dinner at the Four Seasons Hotel – but, in general, the hosts can be proud of their work.

But, amidst this positive picture, there was an elephant in the room, one for which the Saudis bore no responsibility: the veritable ineptitude of arbiters finally became a huge, public embarrassment. The fact of the matter is that arbiting in rapid, and especially blitz chess, is very demanding. Political appointees to the title of International Arbiter (and, shamefully, there are many of those) are, by definition, inadequate to the task. It was a good job that the ginger-haired Australian buffoon and patzer to boot, Jamie Kenmure, was largely restricted to making announcements in his execrable English, rather than interfering with serious games. Infringements and irregularities – accidental or otherwise – happen at lightning pace and sound judgment is required. Unfortunately, even many of the qualified arbiters are found hopelessly wanting. When Ernesto Inarkiev outrageously claimed a win against Magnus Carlsen after he himself had made an illegal move, the match arbiter, Carlos Dias, unbelievably awarded him the point (before being over-ruled by the Chief Arbiter)! Not only did he fail to forfeit Inarkiev for his transgression (OK, Magnus didn't spot it either), but he displayed gross ignorance of the Laws of Chess. Furthermore (and this is almost worse in my view) he didn't apply a shred of common sense. At the very least he should be forced to pass his exams again before he is allowed near a kindergarten event, let alone a world championship.

'Political appointees to the title of International Arbiter (and, shamefully, there are many of those) are, by definition, inadequate to the task.'

Later, there was an incident involving Alexander Grischuk, who correctly claimed a draw by threefold repetition against Shakhriyar Mamedyarov, but was initially denied by IA Mahdi Abdulrahim, who was unable to recognise it. Dare I suggest, as several arbiters have done to me sotto voce, that a minimum level of playing strength should be required to officiate at these events? Ironically, both these experienced referees are members of the mafia known as the FIDE Arbiters' Commission, which tends to protect its own. Reform must obviously come from without, not within. One further important point: if you can afford to spend an alleged $200,000 on a lavish dinner, you can probably afford cameras to cover every board. That will nip many a dispute in the bud. Blitz is now a multi-million dollar business and no longer the sole preserve of park hustlers.

At the opening ceremony, the unhealthy-looking acting FIDE President, Georgios Makropoulos, made an impassioned speech calling on the 2018 championships to be called the 'King Salman Peace and Friendship World Rapid and Blitz Championships'. It almost brought tears to my eyes until I remembered that if they wanted to ensure everyone could play, they could easily have insisted upon it. The funny thing is, I wouldn't be at all surprised if it happens next year: Saudi Arabia is changing and FIDE does not want to risk being sued. And if that is the case, it is going to be a truly great event. If they can find some decent arbiters, that is. ■

The King of Blitz

Useful lessons to be learned from Magnus Carlsen's superb win in the World Blitz Championship.

Magnus Carlsen had a great time at the Blitz World Championship. One of his rare losses (two in total) he suffered against Russia's Sanan Sjugirov.

After the first day of the King Salman Blitz World Championship, he was trailing defending champion Sergey Karjakin by 2(!) full points, but on the second day Magnus Carlsen was merciless, majestic and often machine-like as he reclaimed the crown, a crown not only he himself thinks is rightly his. **MAXIM DLUGY,** a leading blitz authority and a tireless promoter, presents a crash course in blitz and illustrates his rules and his lucid pieces of advice by a crystal clear dissection of the games that secured the Norwegian's triumph.

'The lure of blitz is that if you are sharp, fresh and lucky you can beat anyone in the world.'

When the World Rapid and Blitz Championships were finally announced by FIDE, I was happy. Ever since the first official World Blitz Championship held in 1989 in St. John, Canada, a World Blitz Championship for me has always been first and foremost a celebration of chess! As the best players in the world come together to focus all their knowledge, energy and abilities for five minutes or less – it becomes a display of all their strengths and weaknesses for spectators to admire, analyse and learn from.

This event in Riyadh was glorified by the largest ever prize-fund and darkened by Saudi Arabia's state policy of excluding players from Israel, Qatar, and Iran from participating. Additionally, many top players do not approve of the politics of a state that chooses to suppress certain human rights now considered standard in most countries, and therefore openly voiced their disagreement with FIDE's practice of accepting bids from such venues. Still, to paraphrase a Russian proverb: 'When you can't catch fish, a crab will do' and FIDE, instead of agonizing for the next three years whether to have the World Blitz and Rapid events at all, due to difficulties of finding a sponsor, signed a three-year-contract with Saudi Arabia's King Salman to ensure three well-organized events with excellent prize money ($2 million in total this year) and $1.2 million in fees over three years for itself. There was even serious discussion that players from the three aforementioned countries would be able to get visas somehow, and I am sure that the Saudi Chess Federation really did try (and at the very last moment there were visas for Qatari players) – but it's always hard to get governments to change their minds – just look at poor Kirsan Ilyumzhinov's blacklist status with the United States of America.

Aside from politics, which is really not the chess world's main area of concern, the event was a success! With the exception of the top American trio, most of the best players in the world made it with their visas intact. The first prize in the Blitz Championship was a dazzling $250,000 (minus the FIDE management fee of $50K) with 30 prizes going down to $1000 (or $800 after FIDE tax). That meant that winning or placing high in the event would likely be the biggest payday of the year for many of the players participating. You just had to keep your energy up for two days straight!

The magic

The format was the already tried and proven 21-round Swiss System tournament, with 11 games played on the first day, and 10 on the last one. The lure of blitz is that if you are sharp, fresh and lucky you can beat anyone in the world, and thus 148 players took to it hoping for a nice New Year's present at the end of the marathon. What happened is already history, and I am sure I will not surprise you by telling you that Magnus Carlsen, our World Champion and the highest-rated blitz player in the world, won the event with 16/21 points, 1½ points ahead of Sergey Karjakin and Vishy Anand. Still, the road to this success was paved with surprises and disappointments, and I want to take you down that way, so you can feel the magic behind Carlsen's success and perhaps by using some of his methods become a better blitz player yourself.

10 important ideas

As a former avid blitz player myself, I have a good feel for what it takes to perform well in such events. In my book *Grandmaster Insides*, published about a year ago, I devote a whole chapter to the benefits of playing blitz for becoming a stronger chess player in all time-controls and to the ways to learn to excel at blitz in particular. Below, you will find 10 important ideas to keep in mind, for they will help you to master the subject.

1 Play faster than your opponent – the only way not to lose on time!

2 A minute in a blitz game is equal to a pawn (don't waste time if it won't get you anything).

3 Frequently check how much time both you and your opponent still have, and be ready to change your speed of play based on these findings.

4 Do *not* look at the clock when your opponent is thinking for longer than usual – instead, look immediately after your reply – your opponent will remember about the clock and will play faster if you warn him by checking his time.

5 Try to play in two-move combinations, forcing your opponent to be the first one to stop to think after a combination. If you see a move and the reply is obvious, decide on your second move before moving.

6 Spend about 30 percent on the opening, 40 percent on the

middlegame and 30 percent on the endgame – but do not spend more time than your opponent. Being ahead even 10-15 seconds can become critical when you both get down to the last minute.

7 In practice games, play some 3-minute, 2-minute, 1-minute chess to see the speed you need to be at in those time-controls. *When you get to those times on your clock – adjust your speed to those times.*

8 In *Zombie mode* – when both players have less than 20 seconds on the clock – the position no longer matters – only your speed does. Play as fast as you can – find a piece you can keep moving and move it, or use your rook to check your opponent's king or push a passed pawn. Do not stop to think about anything – it just doesn't matter!

9 Practice mating your opponent quickly with basic mates such as with King and Queen or King and Rook against King. It should take you under 10 seconds to deliver those mates.

10 Find your own rhythm of moving, so that if you know your next move, you start moving your hand when your opponent finishes their move and presses the clock. It will save at least half a second each time – which could add up to half a minute for the game (or half a pawn).

Of course, to become a good blitz player, you also need to play strong moves, but the 10 suggestions above will allow you to play the best blitz possible with the abilities you have right now.

Now let's focus on our champ and see what other key things we can learn from his play.

Magnus Carlsen
Ernesto Inarkiev
Riyadh blitz 3' + 2" 2017 (1)
Sicilian Defence

1.e4 c5 2.a3
Well, now we come to the next important question: How do we prepare for serious blitz? One of the key answers is: learn some cool gambits! With this move, Magnus is clearly signalling that he is preparing b4. As we will see from the next few moves, it will be clear that this was actually part of his preparation for the tournament. Since every minute is a pawn, winning even 30 seconds on the clock by playing an unconventional move is extremely important in blitz. If, in addition, you can force your opponent to defend, it will gain you even more time, since defending is actually a more time-consuming task than attacking, for the simple reason that you must defend, while you can pause your attack with a general purpose move.
2...♘c6 3.b4!

Magnus forges ahead. Unsurprisingly, this gambit is sound enough

not to give Black any advantage, and therefore a perfect choice for blitz!
3...cxb4
Ernesto is a principled player and he has a good feeling for what is playable and what is not, so he did not take much time to accept the gambit. Still, objectively speaking this is probably *not* the correct decision. Since White has spent two moves on playing b4, Black, instead of obliging with the acceptance of the gambit, should simply develop himself with either 3...e5 or 3...e6, with a very nice position.
4.axb4 ♘xb4 5.d4 d5!

> **'I want you feel the magic behind Carlsen's success and perhaps by using some of his methods become a better blitz player yourself.'**

Black is correct to put a foot out into the centre with his pawn, or else White's space advantage will become threatening.
6.c3 ♘c6 7.exd5 ♕xd5 8.♘a3
This move was played in one second, indicating that this was all part of White's preparation. With the obvious moves played, it's now time for Black to decide how to develop his pieces.

8...♗f5
A difficult decision that took Black 45 seconds (or 3/4 of a pawn!). The engines suggest a move that discombobulates White's pieces: 8...♕a5!?,

and after 9.♗d2 ♘f6 10.♗d3 ♕d8 11.♘f3 ♗g4 12.♕e2 e6 it looks like Black is doing quite well.

9.♘b5 ♖c8

The only move, but White is already clearly better! Wow! A nice turn of events, you might say. But this is blitz, and success has to be defended with every move.

10.♘xa7

Magnus took over a minute on this capture, clearly calculating many tactical lines, and now it was Black's turn to check the champ's analysis.

10...♘xa7

Ernesto consumed just over 2 minutes on this forced reply, trying to make the tactics work with alternatives. Let's take a look at what he may have been considering: 10...♖a8 11.♘b5! (threatening 12.♘c7+) 11...♕e4+ 12.♗e3 ♖xa1 13.♕xa1, and White has a very good position thanks to the possible infiltration down the a-file. The queen swap will not help, as after 13...♕b1+ 14.♕xb1 ♗xb1 15.d5 White mobilizes his rook first, with a winning position, e.g. after 15...♘e5 16.♗d4 ♘d7 17.♗c4 ♘h6 18.♘f3 ♘f5 19.0-0 ♘xd4 20.♘bxd4 ♗e4 21.♘g5 ♗g6 22.♖a1.

On 10...♕e6+ 11.♗e3 ♘xa7 12.♖xa7 ♕b6 White can play 13.d5 or even 13.♕a1!, with a far better position.

11.♖xa7 e5

Black correctly avoids 11...♖xc3, as after 12.♕a4+ ♔d8 13.♗d2 ♖b3 14.♗e2 ♖b1+ 15.♗d1 ♘f6 16.♖a8+ ♗c8 17.♖xc8+ ♔xc8 18.♕c2+ White wins.

12.♘f3 exd4

Ernesto Inarkiev sits waiting as Magnus Carlsen arrives, blissfully unaware of the weird turn their game will take.

13.♘xd4!

With Black nearly out of time, Magnus uncharacteristically does not go for a much better endgame in which he could try to press his advantage home, but decides to play practically by keeping more pieces on the board, forcing Inarkiev to find defensive moves with less than 10 seconds on his clock. I am convinced that this was the best decision.

After 13.♕xd4 ♘f6 14.♕xd5 ♘xd5 15.♗b5+ ♔d8 16.♖xb7 ♘xc3 17.0-0 ♘xb5 18.♖xb5 ♗d7 19.♖d5 ♔e8 20.♖e1+ ♗e6 21.♖b5 ♗c5 22.♘g5 ♔d7 23.♘xe6 fxe6 White is, of course, better but it makes Black's defensive task much easier.

13...♗d7! Black has equalized, and now it was up to Magnus to find a way to complicate the position.

14.♘b5?!

Twisting the position, but forcing Black to play without thinking.

14...♕xd1+ 15.♔xd1

With a couple of seconds left, Ernesto has invested the bulk of his time – six seconds - into trading on d1, and Black has to play in the Zombie mode – meaning that no real calculation is possible. Magnus just has to keep his pieces coming out to create new threats and Black should blunder. Let's take a look.

15...♗c6?

A typical mistake. With enough time, it's imaginable that Ernesto, who thrives on counterplay, would find 15...♗c5 16.♖xb7 ♘f6 17.♗d3 0-0, when White has to be careful to fend off Black's multiple threats, including the immediate one of ...♗c6xg2. White would be worse.

16.♗d3 ♗c5 17.♖e1+ ♘e7

18.♗a3!

An excellent counter by Magnus. Black is still fine, but look at what happens next.

18...♗xa3 19.♖xa3 ♖d8 20.♘d4 ♔d7 21.♖a7 ♖he8?! Black keeps equality by kicking out the rook from a7 with 21...♘c8 instead.

22.♔c2 ♔c7 23.♖b1 ♖b8 24.f3 ♘d5?

Finally the Zombie mode has created a real lemon. Black can still hold the position with the modest ...g6, ...h6, or ...♖ed8, but lack of time makes players think they need to lunge at their opponents, creating more problems for themselves.

25.♘xc6 ♔xc6 26.♗b5+ ♔b6

27.♖xb7+

A nice desperado combination. And now, after the expected 27...♖xb7

Magnus Carlsen tells arbiter Carlos Dias that he doesn't understand his decision. Henrik Carlsen and Chief Arbiter Takis Nikolopoulos listen with great interest.

28.♗xe8+ ♔c7 29.♖xb7+ ♔xb7 30.♗xf7 ♘e3+ 31.♔d3 ♘xg2 32.c4, White should have won the pawn-up ending, but that's not what happened. Instead, Zombie mode called and Inarkiev, unhappy with taking on b7, lunged out again with the most amazing 27...♘e3+??!! – the reader can decide on the correct punctuation after hearing the whole story.

Magnus, who did not expect a knight move at all – himself in Zombie mode as well – as his time had finally ticked down to a few seconds, immediately thought about safety and played 28.♔d3??!, reaching the position in the diagram with Black still in check!

Of course, if Magnus had pointed out that Ernesto had made an illegal move, the game would have ended on the spot in White's favour, but instead he moved his king, arguably making an illegal move himself. At this point, Ernesto realized what had happened, stopped the clocks and called the arbiter, claiming that it was White who made the final illegal move, and therefore he deserved to win. The arbiter standing near the game ruled in Black's favour, which led Magnus to question the decision. When a higher arbiter got involved, he ruled that according to the Blitz rules, if a player does not notice that an illegal move has been made and makes a move himself, the game should continue from the new position.

Inarkiev refused to continue and appealed the decision, whereupon Magnus magnanimously offered to split the point. Inarkiev refused and resigned the game when his appeal was rejected basically on the same grounds as the higher arbiter's decision. 1-0 for the World Champ, who also showed that he is a true gentleman.

Cure worse than the disease

As of January 1, 2018, FIDE is trying to change the rules to do away with an immediate loss for an illegal move, applying a minute of extra time to the offended player. Of course, this is a case of a cure being much worse than the disease, since now illegal moves could simply be met by more attacks, followed by pointing out that the player is in check, for instance. This will lead to ridiculous situations. To illustrate the point, imagine play goes: 1.e4 d5 2.♗b5+ h5??, and now it's much more advantageous to play 3.♕xh5! than to request an extra minute, since White is sure to win the rook on h8 in a move or two. Let's hope FIDE actually thinks before it moves on this one to make the rules clear-cut and avoid possible abuse.

One of the most important aspects of a successful blitz tournament performance is the ability to fight on in lost positions, saving and even winning some of them. In this respect, Magnus's speed and technique combine to make him a very difficult player to beat. In this fragment, we take the game from where Magnus blunders away his position against Wang Hao. See how he saves a position that most players would have abandoned as hopeless.

Magnus Carlsen
Wang Hao
Riyadh blitz 3' + 2" 2017 (7)

position after 38.f5

38...♗c8 39.♕h6? ♗xf5 40.♕f4
Magnus just shook off his blunder

and five seconds later he recovered, ready to fight for a draw tooth and nail.
40...♗e6 41.♕f6 ♕e7 42.♕xe7 ♖xe7 43.♘d1

One of the major defensive tools is finding the best stable squares for your pieces. Magnus immediately spots c3 for his knight.
43...♖d7 44.♘c3 ♖d2 45.♖e2
For better or worse, White has no choice.
45...♖xe2 46.♘xe2 ♔g7 47.♔f2 ♔f6 48.♔e3 ♔e5 49.♘g1!
Once again spotting the best square for the knight. Now a new one, since the black king has to be kept out as long as possible.
49...b5 50.♘f3+ ♔d6 51.♔d4
Somehow White has the better king, and now it's time to set up a blockade.
51...a5 52.h4!
As pawns leave the light squares, Black's bishop is losing his targets.

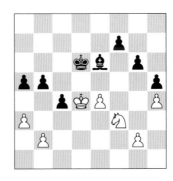

52...b4?
After this the position is just a draw. Black had to prepare a king infiltration with 52...♔c6! 53.♘e5+ ♔b6 54.g3 f5!, and now, after the logical sequence 55.♘xg6 fxe4 56.♔xe4 (56.♘f4 looks stronger, but after 56...♗f7 57.g4 hxg4

58.h5 g3 59.h6 ♗g6 60.♔e5 ♗h7 61.♔d5 a4 Black is also winning) 56...♔c5 57.♘f4 ♗g4 58.♔e3 b4, White is losing.
53.axb4 axb4 54.♘d2 c3 55.bxc3 bxc3 56.♔xc3 ♔e5

57.g3! Magnus stops 57...♔f4, securing a draw.
57...f5 58.♘f3+ Instead of looking to save the position after 58.exf5, which is also drawn, Magnus sees an obvious fortress and goes for it.
58...♔xe4 59.♘g5+ ♔e5
59...♔e3 60.♘xe6 ♔f3 61.♘f4 ♔xg3 62.♘xg6 f4 63.♘xf4 is just another draw.
60.♔d3 ♗d5 61.♔e3 f4+ 62.♔f2 ♔f5 63.♘h3 fxg3+ 64.♔xg3 ♗b7

Draw. Saving games like this adds to one's confidence.

Extremely sound and resolute

Magnus's ability to make something out of nothing even against the world's top players, stems from his basic understanding of sound chess principles. While he often experiments in openings, understanding that the difference between minus a half and plus a half is negligible in blitz, when the middlegame starts transposing to the endgame, he begins to play chess in an extremely sound and resolute manner, building up small advantages and not letting go till he is forced to.

In this example against the super-experienced Vishy Anand, he makes something out of nothing and comes close to outwitting one of the oldest foxes on the circuit.

Vishy Anand
Magnus Carlsen
Riyadh blitz 3' + 2" 2017 (8)
Pirc Defence, Classical Variation

That's what relief looks like. Vishy Anand is happy that he's averted a loss against Magnus Carlsen, who kept looking for his chances in a balanced position.

1.e4 ♘c6
Magnus experiments with this hybrid of the Nimzowitsch and Pirc Defence (together with his second move 2...d6) to force his opponents to feel uneasy about just developing, as there is always a desire to find your way to a slight advantage whenever you are facing a slightly inferior opening. In a blitz game this can result in wasting 30-60 seconds, which is worth a half to a full pawn – making even a successful attempt to find an edge futile. Hikaru Nakamura also endorses this theory and combines ...b6 with ...g6 in blitz games, looking to carry most of the play into the deep middlegame phase.

9.♗f4 If Anatoly Karpov were playing, he would attack with 9.♗f1!, as he did against Pfleger in this

'Magnus makes something out of nothing and comes close to outwitting one of the oldest foxes on the circuit.'

2.♘f3 Vishy does not mind 2...e5, as we can see from this reluctance to play the most principled 2.d4 here. It's nice to see that Vishy took only two seconds for this decision.
2...d6 3.d4 ♘f6 4.d5!
As a matter of principle, White takes space and time to claim a slight edge.
4...♘b8 5.♘c3 g6 6.♗e2 ♗g7 7.0-0 0-0 8.♖e1 c6

position some 40 years back.
9...b5! A timely response, exploiting the weakening of the b2-pawn.
10.a3 After 10.dxc6 b4 11.♘d5 ♘xc6 12.a3 bxa3 13.♖xa3 ♖b8 Black has enough counterplay on the queenside to successfully fight for equality. Vishy prefers prophylaxis.
10...a6 11.♕d2 ♗b7 12.♖ad1 ♘bd7 13.dxc6 ♗xc6

By now it has become clear that the expansion White allowed on the queenside with ♗f4, allowed Magnus to equalize. Vishy decides to eliminate any danger through simplification.
14.e5 dxe5 15.♘xe5 ♘xe5 16.♗xe5 ♕xd2 17.♖xd2 ♖fd8 18.♖xd8+ ♖xd8 19.♖d1 ♖c8
Magnus doesn't mind playing equal positions to see if his colleagues make mistakes. He preserves the rooks to create problems later.
20.♘a2 ♗b7 21.c3 ♘e8 It's quite an interesting fact that Magnus spent one minute and 29 seconds on this move alone, deciding against 21...♘e4. What happens next is quite surprising and shows his will to win at all costs.
22.♗g3 ♘f6 23.♗e5 It was logical to bring in the knight with 23.♘b4 instead, trying to get some pressure

going in the centre or on the queen-side, but Vishy is not interested.

23...♘e4! Magnus spent only seven seconds on this pawn sacrifice, avoiding repetition with 23...♘e8. It seems clear to me that he thought the pawn sac was close the first time around, but then chose the safe route. Now that Anand is showing he can draw at will, he resists and sacrifices first. I am sure that most of the calculation of the sacrifice was done as he was deciding on the move 21...♘e8.
24.♗xg7 ♔xg7 25.♖d7 ♘c5 26.♖xe7 ♔f6 27.♖e3 ♖d8
Black takes over the d-file and the 7th rank, which is just enough compensation. But why do this instead of taking a draw? The answer is below.
28.c4 bxc4 29.♗xc4 ♖d1+ 30.♗f1

30...♖d2? The last serious investment of time by Magnus and a mistake. After a 22-second think Magnus shuns the exact 30...♖b1 31.b4 ♘e4 32.♘c3 ♘xc3 33.♖xc3 a5 34.b5 ♔e5 35.f3 ♔d5 36.♔f2 ♔d4 37.♖c2 ♖a1, with an equal position, since his pieces are extremely active.
31.♖e2 ♖d1 32.♘c3 ♖c1

33.f3?!
It's hard to play this endgame perfectly, but after the correct 33.♖d2 (preparing ♖d1) 33...a5 34.♖d1 ♖c2 35.♖d6+ ♔e7 36.♖b6! ♖c1 37.♘e2 ♖d1 38.♖b5 ♗a6! 39.♖xc5 ♔d6! 40.♖c1 ♗xe2 41.♖xd1+ ♔xd1, White has reasonable winning chances in this pawn-up endgame.
33...a5

34.♔f2?!
This gives up all the advantage still to be had after 34.♖d2 ♗a6 35.♖d1 ♖xd1 36.♘xd1 ♗xf1 37.♔xf1 a4 38.♘c3, although the knight and pawn ending is probably drawn, since Black's king will head for d4.
34...♗a6 35.♖e1 ♖c2+ 36.♔g3 ♗xf1 37.♘d5+ ♔g7 38.♖xf1 ♖xb2

Suddenly it has become clear that White must be very careful if he wants to draw.
39.♖c1 ♘d3 40.♖c3 ♘e1 41.♘e3 ♖e2 42.f4?
An inaccuracy by Vishy, creating undesirable weaknesses.
Instead, 42.h4, giving his king the comfy h3-square, would have kept equality.
42...h5 43.h3 h4+ 44.♔g4

44...f5+?
Magnus throws away all his advantage. After 44...♔h6! White would be lucky to survive after 45.f5 ♘xg2 46.♘c4 ♖f2 (threatening mate in 1) 47.♖f3 ♖c2 48.♘d6 (48.♘xa5? would lose to a simple and elegant zugzwang after, for instance, 48...f6! 49.a4 g5, with a mate in four after the best 50.♖f1 ♖c3 51.♖f3 ♘e3+ 52.♖xe3 ♖xe3 53.♘c6 ♖g3 mate) 48...f6 49.♘f7+ ♔g7 50.♘d6 ♖c6 51.♖d3 g5, and White has to bail out into a knight and pawn ending with 52.♘e4 ♔h6 53.♖d6 ♖xd6 54.♘xd6 ♘e1, which seems lost after the best play.
45.♔g5 ♔f7 46.a4 ♘xg2 47.♘xg2 ♖xg2+ 48.♔xh4
And the players agreed to a draw.

How did Magnus get a nearly winning endgame from a slightly worse position? The answer is: he is not afraid to engage in any kind of position and he does it exuding confidence, which makes his opponents play a little too passively, making mistakes when the time-factor becomes more important.

Shakhriyar Mamedyarov
Magnus Carlsen
Riyadh blitz 3' + 2" 2017 (14)

position after 21...♘xf3+

This completely equal position occurred in Mamedyarov-Carlsen. How can Black win this, you may wonder. Well, not without a little help from our friends, as the Beatles song goes.

22.♕xf3 ♕e7 23.h3 h6 24.b4 ♖c8 25.g3 b6 26.h4 ♕e6 27.♔g2 ♖e8 28.♖d3 ♕e7 29.♕d5 ♕c7 30.♕d7 ♖e7 31.♕d5

It's clear that Mamedyarov is also toying with the idea of playing this position for some strange reason. While this method could prove plausible against lesser players, my feeling is that here simply trading queens and offering a draw was a good way out.

31...♖e8 32.b5 ♕e5 33.♕d7 ♕e4+ 34.♔g1 ♖e5 35.♖d1 ♕f3 36.a4 ♖e4

So, White has weakened his queenside pawns, weakened his h1-a8 diagonal allowing Black's queen to settle nicely into that nook and has now left himself only one move for

equality. All this in a few moves of trying to unsettle the position. Now it's time to go wrong.

37.♕d8+
Already an inaccuracy. It was important to keep an eye on the a7-pawn. After the best 37.♖a1 f5 38.♖c1 ♖e2 39.♖f1 f4 40.♕c8+ ♔h7 41.♕f5+, White draws easily.

37...♔h7

38.♕d5?? Wow! A real lemon! White would be worse after 38.♖a1 ♕c3 39.♕d1 ♖d4 40.♕b1+ ♔g8 41.♖a2 g6, but not enough to even call this more than a tad better for Black. Now it all ends abruptly. **38...♖e1+** 0-1.

Once again, when a player is down to the last 10 seconds, as in this case, it's possible to make a blunder of any magnitude. King safety becomes extremely important, as you have to have the time to calculate all checks. In Zombie mode, that is usually impractical. My advice is to keep your king safer than your opponent's when both of you are approaching the final seconds. It's clear to me that Magnus is well aware of this idea, while his opponents think they can outsmart the

odds and continue to miss key checks when low on time.

The leader of the pack

As Magnus began to pick up speed by beating Grischuk, Harikrishna and Mamedyarov in Rounds 12-14, he was finally in reach of first place when he got paired with the leader of the pack, his last rival for the main title and last year's Blitz World Champion, Sergey Karjakin, who topped the table after Day 1. It was clear that the winner of this game would become the clear favourite in the race to the finish. Magnus won in fine style with this effort.

Magnus Carlsen
Sergey Karjakin
Riyadh blitz 3' + 2" 2017 (15)
Four Knights Defence

1.e4 e5 2.♘f3 ♘c6 3.♗b5 ♘f6 4.d3 ♗c5 5.♗xc6 dxc6 6.♘c3 0-0 7.♗e3 This move, used by Karjakin himself to beat Vladimir Malakhov, has not been seen in Magnus's games. He previously preferred to play 7.h3 or even 7.♘xe5 in this position.
7...♗d6 8.♗g5

A move not seen before in GM games, with 8.h3 being the move of choice.
8...♖e8 9.h3 c5
This looks like a hurried decision. There is no reason for Black to give away his bishop for the knight yet, because White will never play d4. It makes sense to me to take some space on the queenside now with 9... a5, trying to see where White wants to castle and how he will meet Black's

potential expansion on the queenside. In that case, Black's two bishops should easily compensate for the slightly damaged pawn structure.

10.♘d5!

Magnus immediately takes the opportunity to get a little edge by forcing the exchange of his knight for the bishop.

10...♗e7 11.♘xe7+ ♕xe7 12.0-0 h6 13.♗e3

Magnus relieves the pressure on the knight and allows Black a typical equalizing manoeuvre, which Sergey ignores. It was better to play for f4 with the bishop on h4. After 13.♗h4 ♕d6 14.♘d2 ♘h7 15.♗g3 ♗e6 16.b3 ♘f8 17.f4 exf4 18.♗xf4, White is a tad better.

The old and the new Blitz World Champions, Sergey Karjakin and Magnus Carlsen, at the closing ceremony amid chess officials and local dignitaries.

13...♘d7?! Sergey starts a typical knight manoeuvre to sustain White's central advance, but it takes a bit too long. Meanwhile after the straightforward 13...c4! Black has a very comfortable position. Sergey took only five seconds for this move, a clear indication that he is playing cliché moves instead of looking for an opportunity in a slightly different position from what he is used to.

14.♘d2 ♘b8

15.f4 As we say in a number of countries, 'Strike the iron while it's hot'. Magnus puts pressure on Black's kingside, while Black is repositioning his knight.

15...exf4 16.♖xf4 ♘c6 17.♕h5 b6 18.♖af1

The attack is playing itself. Black's position is weakened by the pawn on h6 and therefore not as impregnable as Sergey probably thought.

18...♖f8

19.♘f3

Magnus took 36 seconds for this move, but objectively the strongest way to reinforce the attack was 19.♖4f3!, immediately pointing the

e3-bishop to the target on h6. After 19...♕e5 20.♕h4 ♘d4 White can win a pawn with 21.♖xf7 ♖xf7 22.♕d8+ ♔h7 23.♖xf7 ♘xc2 24.♗f4 ♕d4+ 25.♕xd4 ♘xd4 26.♗e5 ♘e6 27.♖e7, followed by ♗xc7, or opt to continue his attack with 21.♖3f2!.

19...♗e6 20.♖h4 f6 21.♕g6

21...♕f7?

A serious mistake. Black had a fully defensible position after 21...♗f7 22.♕g3 ♔h7, creating the kind of impregnable dark-squared fortress Sergey was hoping for. Now Magnus opens up Black's position like a can of sardines.

22.♕g3

22...♞b4?

It took Sergey 44 seconds to come up with this method of traditional seppuku. The only possible way to continue defending was 22...h5, sacrificing a pawn to fend off the immediate threats after 23.♗h6 ♖ad8 24.♖xh5 ♖d7 25.♖h4 c4, when White's most decisive continuation 26.dxc4 ♗xc4 27.♗xg7 ♕xg7 28.♖g4 ♗xf1 29.♔xf1 ♞e5 30.♖xg7+ ♖xg7 31.♕f4 ♞xf3, would still require some good technique from the World Champ.

23.♗xh6 ♞xc2

24.♞e5!

The final phase of the game is upon us. The one that's usually called curtains.

24...fxe5 25.♖xf7 ♖xf7 26.♕g6 ♗xa2 27.♗g5 ♖ff8 28.♖h7 ♖f7 29.♗f6

And Sergey resigned.

One cannot escape the feeling that when Magnus is given a chance to pounce, he is ready to do it quickly and confidently. With this win Magnus took the lead in the tournament that he had started building up to round by round.

Watch the pawn on g4

In the following game, played in the 17th round, Magnus gets attacked early in the opening after Tigran Petrosian sacrifices a piece for a few pawns. Amazingly, Magnus manages to defend this difficult position and eventually take over the initiative with seeming ease, displaying his prowess at finding the best manoeuvres with his knights, while also pressing on time.

Final times for this game: Petrosian, four seconds remaining, Magnus 1 minute 28 seconds!

Tigran Petrosian
Magnus Carlsen
Riyadh blitz 3' + 2" 2017 (17)
Réti Opening

1.♞f3 c5 2.g3 g6 3.♗g2 ♗g7 4.0-0 ♞c6 5.e4 d6 6.d3 e5

A very sound strategy against both the English and the Closed Sicilian is to focus Black's attention on the d4-square – the square White is seeming to ignore with his setup. After that, Black's typical plan is to expand on the queenside, putting pressure on White's position before he sets his eyes on attacking Black's king.

7.c3 ♞ge7 8.a3 0-0 9.b4 a6 10.♞bd2 ♗e6

A slight inaccuracy, allowing White the surprising sacrificial idea that occurred in the game. It would have been more prudent to play the prophylactic 10...h6!, stopping the ♞g5 lunge for good.

11.♞g5! ♗d7 12.♞c4! h6?

This is an outright mistake, allowing White a nasty follow-up. Magnus had to take a time-out with ...♗c8 or ...♞c8, followed by ...h6, before restarting his play in the centre. Now White has an excellent opportunity.

13.♞xd6?!

Strong, but not the best! After 13.♞xf7 ♖xf7 14.♞xd6, White simply wins material, with a great game. Even after the sturdiest defence 14...cxb4 15.♞xf7 ♔xf7 16.axb4 ♗e6 17.♗e3 ♔g8 18.♕d2 h5 19.f4 Black would be in serious trouble, as White's united pawn front is very difficult to stop.

13...hxg5 14.♞xb7 ♕c8 15.♞xc5

15...g4! An excellent positional move by Magnus, who blocks the advance of White's pawns while protecting his g-pawn. Now the position is still better for White, but playing it well requires guts.

16.♗g5 ♖e8 17.♕b3?

This logical looking move is a significant mistake. White should not have placed the queen where White's knight may need to retreat, and should have looked to prepare d4 with ♖c1 instead. After 17.♖c1 a5 18.f4 gxf3 19.♕xf3 f6 20.♗e3 ♘d8 21.d4 ♘f7 22.♕e2 White has a very strong initiative, as all his pieces are put to work, especially the rook on f1.

17...♘d8!

A superb manoeuvre by Magnus, looking to get rid of White's strongest minor piece – the knight on c5.

18.♗e3 ♘e6 19.♖fd1?!

An inaccuracy. To keep the balance, White should get rid of Black's b7-bishop, which will otherwise look to invade on Tigran's light squares. After 19.♘xd7 ♕xd7 20.♖ad1 ♖ac8 21.f3!, getting rid of the clamp on the kingside, the position is complicated but balanced.

19...♘xc5

20.♗xc5?

Tigran should have banked on the power of his pawns and played 20.bxc5. Now, after 20...♖b8 21.♕c2 ♗c6 22.d4 ♕d7 23.d5 ♗a4 24.♕e2 ♗xd1 25.♖xd1, White would have real chances for serious counterplay with his massive pawn complex.

20...♗e6 21.♕a4 ♘c6

As you can see now, the g4-pawn is ruining White's chances for real counterplay, as it basically controls the entire kingside. White is worse and seriously behind on the clock.

22.d4 ♗c4! The bishop finds an excellent outpost on c4. Now it's time to deploy the knight.

23.d5 ♘b8!

24.♗f1? It's understandable that White wants to get his pawns moving, but starting with the a-pawn, although more modest, was a stronger approach. After 24.♕c2 ♘d7 25.♗e3 ♘f6 26.a4 ♕d7 27.f3

♖ac8 28.♖e1, breaking down White's position would be a difficult task.

24...♗xf1 25.♖xf1 ♘d7 26.♗e3 ♘f6! 27.♕b3 ♘xe4 28.c4

The pawns are finally mobile, but Black has recovered a pawn and is now officially up material.

28...♕f5 One very important aspect of Magnus's play in blitz is that he never plays a better position in a risky way. Trying to pry White's kingside open with f5, allowing counterplay, is something he would automatically

'Final times: Petrosian, four seconds remaining, Magnus 1 minute 28 seconds!'

reject. 'Safe is sound' is a very good motto for blitz.

29.♖ac1 ♗f6 30.c5 ♔g7

With nice manoeuvring, Magnus is preparing a mating attack along the h-file.

31.f3

31...♘g5? It was stronger to open up the position with 31...gxf3 32.♖xf3, and now not blundering the queen with 32...♕xf3?? 33.♗h6+!, but playing 32...♕g4, starting to line up the pieces for the attack.

32.♗xg5! ♗xg5 33.♖ce1?
Preparing to push on with the pawns would have been stronger. After 33.♖cd1 e4 34.f4 ♗d8 35.d6 e3 36.♖fe1 e2 37.♖d5 ♕e4 38.♕d3, White is doing fine.

33...gxf3 34.♖xf3 ♕d7 35.d6 e4

36.♕c3+? Of course it is nearly impossible to figure out what's important with less than 10 seconds left. It turns out that the queen needs access to d5 to help the pawns.
After 36.♖ff1 ♖e5 37.c6 ♕xc6 38.♕xf7+ ♔h6 39.h4 ♕xd6 40.hxg5+ ♖xg5 41.♕f4 ♕xf4 42.♖xf4 ♖xg3+ 43.♔h2 ♖xa3 44.♖exe4, White has good chances for survival.

36...♔g8 37.♖f2 Again, keeping the rook out of harm's way with 37.♖ff1 was better. **37...e3**

38.♖f3? The decisive mistake. Now Black's pieces enter with tempo. After 38.♖c2 it would still have been a fight.
38...♕c6! 39.♔g2 ♕d5 40.♖e2 a5! Notice how effortlessly Magnus piles up the pressure from all directions.

41.h4 axb4 42.axb4 ♖a2!
43.♕e1 ♖xe2+ 44.♕xe2

44...♖a8!
With over half his time on the clock, it still takes him only four or five seconds per move to play this nice intermezzo combination.
45.♔h3 ♖a2 46.♕f1 e2 47.♕f2 ♕e6+ And White resigned.

Meeting again

After receiving a serious beating at Magnus's hands during the recent Champions Showdown in St. Louis, Ding Liren cannot have been very confident playing the World Champion again, although he continued to put up tough resistance for a long time. We pick it up from the following position, when Black's activity just about compensates for White's dominance on the queenside. But how can Black win?

Ding Liren
Magnus Carlsen
Riyadh blitz 3' + 2" 2017 (18)

position after 34.♔h1

34...♘e5 35.b5 ♘c4 36.♔g1
♘xe3 37.fxe3 ♕e6 38.a4 ♕b3

39.♕e1
If White was worried about his king, he could have picked up the h3-pawn, but how simple is it? After 39.♕xh3 ♕xe3+ there is only one move that leads to a draw – and it's the least obvious move of the three. That's right, only 40.♔g2 draws, as 40.♔f1 loses after 40...♕c1+ 41.♔e2 ♕c2+ 42.♔e3 ♕d3+ 43.♔f2 e3+ 44.♔f3 g5! (stopping the perpetual check and threatening 45...e2+, followed by 46...♕d2), and after 40.♔h1 ♕c1+ 41.♔g2 ♕c2+! (covering the c8 checking square) 42.♔g1 e3 Black will queen the e-pawn and win.

39...♕xa4 40.♕b1

40...♕a5!
It took Magnus only four seconds to come up with this brilliant winning attempt, preparing a trap for White's planned b6.

41.b6? And White falls for it. It's easy to criticize and claim that White is drawing with reasonable moves like 41.♕c1 or 41.♔f1 or 41.♕d1, but when you have only three or four seconds left, try to take your hand off the b-pawn that you think will save the day. Ding Liren couldn't!

41...♕d2!

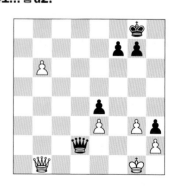

Ding Liren had to try and forget his recent blitz catastrophe against Magnus Carlsen in St. Louis. Easier said than done.

♗e7 8.♗d3 ♘c6 9.a3 0-0 10.0-0 cxd4 11.cxd4

Magnus is not seeking complications. He will play logical, forward-moving chess, forcing his opponent to play well throughout. For a while Korobov keeps pace.

11...♖c8 12.♕e2 ♘h5 13.♗xe7 ♕xe7 14.♖ac1 ♘f6 15.♖c2

Magnus really doesn't care for any complications. He has decided to trade rooks down the c-file before taking control of the centre.

After the more natural 15.e4, White would enjoy a slight advantage, as the threat of creating an attack on the kingside with e5 would be unpleasant.

15...♖b8 16.♖fc1 ♖xc2 17.♖xc2 ♖c8 18.♖xc8+ ♗xc8 19.e4 ♗b7 20.e5

The main motto of blitz play should be to get positions that you can't lose but might win. In this case, if you are leading the event by two points with two rounds to go, it makes sense to do just that.

20...♘h7?

A strange decision by Anton: relinquishing control of the d6-square.

Now Black wins everything, and then the queen and pawn ending as well.

42.♕f1 ♕xe3+ 43.♕f2 ♕c1+ 44.♕f1 ♕c5+ 45.♕f2 e3 46.♕e2 ♕xb6 47.♔f1 ♕b1+ 48.♕e1 ♕e4 49.♔e2 ♕g2+ 50.♔xe3 ♕xh2 51.♔f4 ♕c2

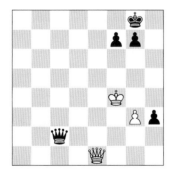

Notice how safely Magnus plays, controlling the b1-h7 diagonal.

52.g4 ♕c7+ 53.♔f3 ♕c6+ 54.♔g3 ♕g2+ 55.♔f4 h2

And White resigned.

Magnus created play out of thin air, able to navigate tactical nuances when the Zombie mode set in.

How can we learn to do the same? My suggestion is to play bullet and

0 2 chess, where you will be forced to make a move in under two seconds on average on an ongoing basis. After a while, you will learn to do some things much faster than you used to. You simply won't have a choice.

The final times, again

The Champ's final win in the event came in Round 20, when he already had clinched the title. Magnus plays a nice positional game, using his slight advantage to continue to put pressure on Anton Korobov until the Ukrainian GM makes a mistake, missing a draw in a knight and pawn ending. The final times of the players show the reason why Magnus wins these seemingly even positions: Magnus 1:19, Korobov five seconds left.

Magnus Carlsen
Anton Korobov
Riyadh blitz 3' + 2" 2017 (20)
Queen's Pawn Opening,
Torre Variation

1.d4 ♘f6 2.♘f3 e6 3.♗g5 c5 4.c3 h6 5.♗h4 b6 6.e3 ♗b7 7.♘bd2

Riyadh 2017 blitz

1	Magnus Carlsen	NOR	2986	16	2924
2	Sergey Karjakin	RUS	2854	14½	2873
3	Vishy Anand	IND	2736	14½	2844
4	Wang Hao	CHN	2737	14	2832
5	Levon Aronian	ARM	2863	14	2794
6	Ding Liren	CHN	2837	13½	2812
7	Tigran Petrosian	ARM	2705	13½	2803
8	Yu Yangyi	CHN	2701	13½	2803
9	Anton Korobov	UKR	2760	13½	2799
10	Shakhriyar Mamedyarov	AZE	2770	13½	2783
11	Peter Svidler	RUS	2797	13½	2784
12	Maxime Vachier-Lagrave	FRA	2853	13	2822
13	Alexander Grischuk	RUS	2725	13	2767
14	Boris Savchenko	RUS	2619	13	2731
15	Hrant Melkumyan	ARM	2686	13	2727
16	Le Quang Liem	VIE	2771	13	2731
17	Rauf Mamedov	AZE	2755	13	2701
18	Ahmed Adly	EGY	2678	13	2672
19	Alexey Dreev	RUS	2640	12½	2751
20	Bassem Amin	EGY	2655	12½	2750
21	Ian Nepomniachtchi	RUS	2810	12½	2751
22	Vidit Gujrathi	IND	2651	12½	2740
23	Vladislav Artemiev	RUS	2798	12½	2734
24	Peter Leko	HUN	2790	12½	2713
25	Pentala Harikrishna	IND	2759	12½	2715
26	Li Chao	CHN	2668	12½	2697
27	Bu Xiangzhi	CHN	2688	12½	2655
28	Wang Yue	CHN	2686	12½	2649
29	Levan Pantsulaia	GEO	2679	12½	2635
30	Baadur Jobava	GEO	2585	12	2778
31	Richard Rapport	HUN	2600	12	2767
32	Sanan Sjugirov	RUS	2645	12	2739
33	Vladimir Fedoseev	RUS	2629	12	2720
34	Etienne Bacrot	FRA	2621	12	2707
35	Sergei Zhigalko	BLR	2586	12	2721
36	Olexandr Bortnyk	UKR	2677	12	2717
37	Giga Quparadze	GEO	2654	12	2688
38	Saleh Salem	UAE	2757	12	2688
39	Viktor Laznicka	CZE	2681	12	2637
40	Ruslan Ponomariov	UKR	2711	12	2608
41	Andrey Esipenko	RUS	2581	11½	2765
42	Laurent Fressinet	FRA	2608	11½	2743
43	Zaven Andriasian	ARM	2755	11½	2700
44	Alexandr Rakhmanov	RUS	2558	11½	2645
45	Paco Vallejo	ESP	2662	11½	2663
46	Varuzhan Akobian	USA	2655	11½	2641
47	Rustam Kasimdzhanov	UZB	2750	11½	2648
48	Ivan Saric	CRO	2674	11½	2588
49	Andrei Volokitin	UKR	2618	11½	2546
50	Farrukh Amonatov	TJK	2628	11	2701
51	Yuriy Kryvoruchko	UKR	2596	11	2717
52	Vladimir Onischuk	UKR	2607	11	2699
53	David Howell	ENG	2571	11	2687

time-control: 3' + 2"

138 players, 21 rounds

20...♘e8 was the most natural and strongest option.
21.♘c4 ♘f8 22.♘d6 ♗xf3 23.♕xf3 ♘c6

24.♕e4?! An inaccuracy that gives Black a chance to equalize.

After 24.♕e3! White will use the e4-square for the bishop to continuously threaten to trade it for the c6-knight, followed by ♘c8 if Black swaps the queens. The endgame would be difficult for Black to play. For example, after 24...♕g5 25.♗e4 ♕xe3 26.fxe3 ♘g6 27.♗xc6 dxc6 28.♘c8 ♔f8 29.♘xa7 ♘e7 30.b4 ♔e8 31.b5, Black is in trouble.

24...f5?! Activating the queen with 24...♕g5! was far stronger.
Now, after 25.♕e3, the extra tempo comes in handy, as Black gets excellent play with 25...♕g4.
It seems White would have to play 25.♕f3, with a balanced game after either 25...f5 or 25...♕c1+ 26.♗f1 ♘xd4 27.♕xf7+ ♔h7 28.g3 ♘g6 29.♘e4 h5 30.♘f6+ ♔h6 31.♘e8 ♘e2+ 32.♔g2 ♘ef4+ 33.gxf4 ♘h4+ 34.♔g3 ♘f5+ 35.♔g2 ♘h4+, with perpetual check.
25.♕e3 ♕h4

26.f4
An inaccuracy from Carlsen, played quickly. The position is actually quite complicated and the inclusion of some intermediate moves could prove White's advantage after the non-trivial 26.♘b5! a6 27.g3 ♕g4 28.f3!. Now, after the strongest sequence 28...f4 29.♕f2 ♕g5 30.♘d6, White has defended his d-pawn and can claim a slight advantage after 30...fxg3 31.hxg3 ♕c1+ 32.♔g2 ♕d1 33.♕e3.
26...g5! 27.g3!
After a 41-second think Magnus decides against capturing on g5, correctly calculating that he will be able to hold the f4-pawn. After 27.fxg5 ♕xg5 28.♕xg5+ hxg5 29.♘b5 ♘g6!, Black would threaten to win both central pawns with ...a6, leaving him with an advantage.
27...gxf4 28.gxf4 ♘g6 29.♕g3!
The move Magnus had to foresee in order to go for this endgame.

29...♔h7?!
Anton quickly decides against winning the d-pawn, but that's not wrong.
After the immediate 29...♕xg3+ 30.hxg3 ♘xd4 31.♘c8 ♘c6 32.♗e2

♘ge7 33.♘d6, White would have enough compensation for the pawn, but no more. Instead, Magnus can now get the edge with optimum play.

30.d5
Played after only a nine-second think, this move gives Black a great saving resource. The immediate 30.♕xh4 ♘xh4 31.d5 would have been stronger, transposing to the game continuation.

Passionate about blitz like few others. Maxim Dlugy plays blitz at the Arkady Dvorkovich Chess Club in 2011 under the watchful eye of Sergey Karjakin and Hikaru Nakamura.

30...♘ce7? It looks as if Korobov actually considered the correct 30...♘cxe5, since he took 34 seconds for his move. Somehow he couldn't make it work. In fact, this move would have saved the day.
Let's take a look: 30...♘cxe5 31.fxe5 ♕d4+ 32.♔f1 ♘f4! 33.dxe6 dxe6, and now

ANALYSIS DIAGRAM

– the safest continuation is 34.♗xf5+ exf5 35.♕g7+ ♔xg7 36.♘xf5+ ♔g6 37.♘xd4 ♘d3, with equality.
– 34.♗c2 ♕xe5 35.♘e8 ♕b5+ 36.♔f2 ♕xb2 37.♕xf4 ♕xc2+, and White cannot effectively hide from checks.
– 34.♗c4 ♕d1+ 35.♔f2 ♕d4+ 36.♔f3 ♘g6! 37.♗xe6 ♕d3+ 38.♔g2

♕e2+, with perpetual check no matter where White goes.
31.dxe6 dxe6 32.♕xh4 ♘xh4 33.♗c4 ♘hg6 34.♗xe6 ♘xf4 35.♗xf5+ ♘xf5 36.♘xf5

36...♔g6 Of course, playing this endgame with only a few seconds on your clock, as in Anton's case, is very difficult. The most resolutely drawn line can be found with a prophylactic move that would be difficult to find even in a normal time-control: 36...a6!! 37.♘e3 ♘d3 38.e6 ♔g6 39.b3 ♔f6 40.♘d5+ ♔xe6 41.♘xb6 ♔e5!, and Black's king is active enough to secure a draw.
37.♘d6?

Magnus surrenders his advantage with this move. After the correct 37.♘e7+ ♔f7 38.♘c8 ♘d3 39.b3 ♔e6 40.♘xa7 ♔xe5 41.♘c8 b5 42.♘a7 ♘c1 43.♘xb5 ♘xb3 44.♔g2, he could get a similar endgame to what he got in the game after Black's mistake.
37...♘d3 38.♘c8

38...♘xe5? Korobov took two seconds for this incorrect capture. Logically, his king is covering the e-pawn, so he should have been concerned with the queenside pawns instead. After 38...♘xb2 39.♘xa7 ♘c4 40.a4 ♔f5 it's a dead draw.
39.♘xa7 ♘c4 40.♘c8!

'Studying endgames and games of Capablanca, Rubinstein, Karpov and, of course, Magnus, will get you closer to where he is!'

Therein lies the problem. Black does not win the pawn on the queenside, because White keeps biting at the b-pawn with his knight.

40...b5?

A further mistake, aggravating the problem. Black's defence lay in bringing the king to help his knight as soon as possible. After the best 40...♔f6 41.a4 ♔e6 42.b3 ♔d7! 43.♘a7 ♘b2 44.♔f2 ♘d3+ 45.♔g3 ♘c5, Black still draws.

41.♘a7 ♘xb2 42.♘xb5

The position is still a draw according to the table bases, but very hard to play when your opponent has 90 seconds, you have five and he is the best technical player in the world. Let's see when and how Black loses from here.

42...♔f5 43.♔g2

43...h5?

Finally the losing move. Moving the pawn closer to the king turns out to be

the decisive mistake, losing precious time Black simply doesn't have. Correct was 43...♘c4 or 43...♔e5, moving the pieces to attack the a-pawn. Generally, Black's drawing plan consists of moving the king to the kingside to win the a-pawn, and then using the knight to take care of White's h-pawn. It's not simple, but doable. Now it's over, with a laconic 'Mate in 38', according to all the engines out there!

44.♔g3 ♔g5 45.♘c3 ♘c4 46.a4 ♘a5 47.♘e4+ ♔g6 48.♔f4 ♘c4 49.♘c5 ♘a5 50.h4 ♔f6 51.♘e4+ ♔g6 52.♘g3

With the h-pawn fixed and under attack, Magnus can simply walk over to make mincemeat out of the knight on the queenside.

52...♘b7 53.♔e3 ♘d6 54.♔d4 ♘b7 55.♔c4 ♔f6 56.♔b4 ♔e5 57.♘xh5 ♔f5 58.♘g3+ And since his knight cannot stop both pawns, Black resigned.

Magnus entered the last round two points ahead of the competition, made a quick draw with Aronian and pocketed $200,000! Way to go champ!

Summing up

If we analyse Magnus's success in blitz, we will find the following key factors:

1 Speed: Out of 21 games, he was down on time only against Yu Yangyi and that was because he took a few seconds to resign a position he had had a very tough time defending. In half the games he had 1 to 1.5 minutes left on the clock when the game ended.

2 Conversion ratio: When Magnus is ahead in a technical position, his technique borders on table base accuracy. He simply knows why bad positions are bad and what is needed to finish off his opponents. Studying endgames and games of Capablanca, Rubinstein, Karpov and, of course, Magnus, will get you closer to where he is!

3 Defensive abilities: When in trouble, Magnus understands which pieces need to stay on the board and which need to be traded, being able to extract himself from the most difficult positions.

4 Preparation: Magnus knows his opening systems very well and when he plays an offbeat line, he is sure to have a positional or tactical trap lined up lest you relax in thinking you are on even ground. My advice is to prepare some gambit or sharp opening lines for your blitz escapades to put pressure on your opponents as well.

5 Nerves: I was amazed to see how quickly Magnus reacted after blundering a healthy pawn to Wang Hao, continuing to play quickly and confidently, and eventually securing a draw. Not being fazed by a mistake is extremely important in a blitz game, since you simply don't have time for emotions when every second counts.

I wish you a Happy New Year and Steady Blitz Play Improvement trailing our Champ!

I would also like to take this opportunity to congratulate Magnus personally on showing himself the *King of Blitz*! ∎

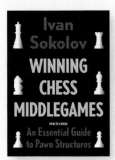
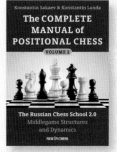

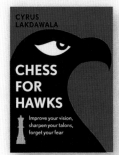
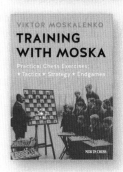

Back at the board

Who hasn't felt the uneasiness of playing after a prolonged break? The rustiness, the lack of rhythm and confidence... As he is mostly absorbed by his academic career these days, with little time left for playing chess, **PARIMARJAN NEGI** can speak from experience. Fortunately, he also has some good advice.

Last year, I played for the Indian national team at the World Team Championship in Khanty-Mansiysk, Russia. This was my first serious event after almost two years. My preparation consisted of thinking about some basic psychological rules, like the ones I have discussed before in my New In Chess columns. For instance, the use of visualizing your move before you make it (in issue 2015/4) or when to calculate (2015/2). Perhaps the best preparation was to solve some tactical positions or play a few blitz games online. But this article focuses on how you can perform better after a long break once you are at the tournament.

Of course, I did not have any illusions about playing at my best. When playing again after a period of inactivity, you should not even worry about your playing strength. There are nicer things to focus on instead. For me, for example, the competitive nature of the game felt like a refreshing break from academics.

As the championship progressed, I began to reflect on how the event

was going. Some things actually worked out well – I played more sensible and calm chess than before. But there were a few recurring psychological mistakes that I noticed. I think these are actually pretty common among people who play rarely – and also not as hard to solve if you become aware of them.

Choosing openings

It is obvious that your tactics may not be as good as before – but your memory will be even worse. So be smart with your choice of openings. Trying to remember the latest trends in the Najdorf won't do you any good. If you don't have any good solid lines in your repertoire, then just look up a few games in a sub-line. For instance, the Scandinavian with ...♕d6 is a perfectly playable solid line, and it takes almost no time to prepare. I just stuck with the Berlin Defence. It seemed like not much had changed there in the last two years, and it was solid enough to not put strains on my memory.

You are not going to get mated

We are all naturally inclined to think more easily of attacking possibilities than defensive ones. In my first game in

Khanty-Mansiysk, I spent a great deal of time right after the opening, almost paranoid about the various threats that he could construct against my king.

Mateusz Bartel
Parimarjan Negi
Khanty-Mansiysk 2017

position after 14.♘c4

This is a fairly standard position. I have played it many times with both colours. White is planning a typical f4 break in order to generate play on the kingside, but Black's position does not have any apparent weaknesses. However, I began to sink into deep thought here. Somehow, I was really afraid of the structure after f4 – exf4 – ♗xf4 – ♖xf4. I was worried that White's play would just be so easy – bring in the other rook to f-file, maybe play ♖f5-♖h5, and then the c4-knight can come to f5, and suddenly it looked as if Black's solid kingside would easily collapse. To be honest, these ideas were not completely pointless. I still believe that White might have slightly better chances with the kind of plans I described, while it isn't immediately clear how Black should generate counterplay. But it is far from simple for White, too, of course – and it took me a long time to convince myself of that. Black would have some counterplay in the centre as well. Most importantly, there isn't much else Black can do. It was obvious to me, based on my experience, that I should go for the positions after ...exf4, as other moves would just give White a very easy initiative after simply playing f5 etc. In short, there was no need to be so paranoid about the kind of problems that might occur in the distant future – especially since I knew there wasn't much else I could do.

14...♘f8 15.f4 exf4 16.♗xf4 ♗xf4 17.♖xf4 ♔h8

Finally, after spending a lot of time, I went for this, correctly deciding that there was no need to commit myself with ...♘g6 yet.

18.e5?

Bartel did not think White had particularly great chances here. He considered Black's position to be a typical solid position, and so he tried to do something immediate. This was a huge relief to me, as I was still afraid about White playing simple improving moves and then checkmating me on the kingside.

I had been afraid of something like 18.♖af1, when I intended to play 18...♕d7 (after repeating my calculations a few times I had convinced myself that e5 was not dangerous because of ...♘g6! – after 18...♘g6 comes 19.♖f5, and then ♖h5 seemed kind of annoying to me). But then 19.♔h1! bothered me somewhat. It wasn't clear to me what I was going to do next. I could push the pawns on the queenside, but that seemed vague and hard to calculate. On the other hand, White has ideas like ♘e3-♘f5, possi-

'Even if you are worried about some lines, **you need to consider too, how it is for your opponent.'**

bly bringing the f4-rook into the attack on the kingside (♖g4/♖h4 etc). I have not analysed this position in depth, but it seems to me that White has the slightly better chances. But if you think about it – it isn't easy for White to play good moves either. And Black can just play slightly improving moves like ...♖ad8 – waiting for White to commit himself to some plan and then trying to fight back against it. When you think about it, it is obvious that White does not have any crushing threats, and it will be a slow strategic battle. This was probably why Bartel did not think his position was too great, since White's main advantage here seems to be that Black won't find it easy to improve his position, whereas White has some potential for a kingside initiative.

This highlights an interesting point. Not having played for so long, I think I had forgotten that we need to also consider our opponent's psychology. Even if you are worried about some lines, you need to consider, too, how it is for your opponent. Here, for instance, I should have realized that it isn't too easy for White either, and the position is sufficiently open and fluid to allow Black chances to generate counterplay.

18...f5!

I think Black is very comfortable now: I can even defend the f5-pawn with ...g6 and play ...♘e6 next, and I like my position a lot more than before White had played e5. The computer does not think there has been such a dramatic shift, but I think that, practically speaking, this position is just nicer for Black. Now we had a fairly complicated middlegame and somehow I survived the tension, even coming close to winning near the end of the game.

Initially, I blamed my insecurity on just being rusty, but then I noticed that it happened in several games. Even the slightest hints of an attack made me start seeing ghosts of mates. But just being aware of it can remedy this problem. A few months after the World Team Championship, I played an invitational rapid in San Francisco with a bunch of local GMs. In the next game, I actually provoked my opponent into going after my king. Once again, the attack looked dangerous at first, but after delving a little deeper it was easy to see that I had decent chances to parry it.

Daniel Naroditsky
Parimarjan Negi
San Francisco (rapid) 2017

position after 16.cxd4

This seems a standard position, with the only anomaly being White's bishop on g3. But the bishop can actually prove useful for White if he gets in something like ♘b5-♘d6, so I decided to deal with this right away.

16...♗xa3! Of course my main worry about giving up the bishop was that the kingside seems to be much more exposed; White will probably soon go ♘g5, potentially followed by f4-f5. It seemed to me that Black should have decent chances to hold by just putting the knight on f8. Meanwhile, Black can start counterplay on the c-file, so it felt like worth the risk. Crucial was that, although I was not sure about this move, and unlike the game with Bartel that we saw, I realized that there would probably be resources in the future, even though I didn't see them at that point.

17.bxa3?

I think the main reason behind this mistake was that Daniel Naroditsky overestimated his attacking chances. For him, getting in ♕d3, ♘g5 and f4-f5 quickly seemed very strong, so he thought he could afford to ignore the queenside completely. In addition, the pawn on a3 prevents annoying moves like ...♘b4.

I had been planning to meet 17.♖xa3 with the same set-up: 17...♖c8 18.♘g5 ♘f8, but here White has additional options because the rook can join the attack. Also, since he hasn't yet spoilt the queenside structure, he may still decide to go for safety if the attack fails.

17...♖c8 18.♘g5 ♘f8! 19.♕d3 ♖a7 20.f4 h6 21.♘f3 ♘e7!

The knights completely block White's attack, and somehow Black is also in time to take over on the queenside. White is already too committed on the kingside, and Daniel continued to try and make it work:

22.♘h4 ♕c7

Just threatening ...♕c2 after f5. The queen swap would lead to a very unpleasant endgame for White.

23.♖ab1 ♕c3 24.♕d1 ♕xa3 25.♖xb6 ♖ac7 26.♘f3 ♖c2 27.♗f2 ♕xa4

And eventually I won the game without many problems.

Do not repeat calculations

Before Khanty-Mansiysk I found myself wondering: what if I was just careful enough to not make any calculating errors? All I would have to do was check my calculations a couple of times whenever the position looked critical. Calculating lines several times is one of the most common ways to deal with a lack of practice. Or perhaps it is just a result of being too rusty. In general, it makes a lot of sense. Should not be too hard, right?

Occasionally, it is certainly good to calculate lines a couple of times, especially if you are particularly rusty. But this can easily take on obsessive proportions, as happened with me. The following story kept repeating itself: I played good moves, but each of these moves in the complications was a hugely stressful affair. And once the 40th move was made, I felt like I could finally relax, that I had pulled through. But despite the extra 30 minutes, I was drained – unable to distinguish fact from fiction – and the stress of repeating my calculations so many times had blurred my vision.

**Vladimir Fedoseev
Parimarjan Negi**
Khanty-Mansiysk 2017

position after 32.♘b3

Despite the early queen swap, this had been a pretty tense endgame so far. Fedoseev had been outplaying me from what looked like nothing, and I was beginning to worry about my position. So in the end I decided to take a more

aggressive stance and went for some forced lines to escape from the slow suffering.

32...♘c3 33.♖e1 ♘a2!?

White's pieces and structure are nicer, so Black should act as fast as he can. At the same time, these forced lines were quite stressful – before playing ...♘a2, I had to calculate the position after 36.b6 ♖c3. The trouble was that I was still not confident in my calculations – whereas Fedoseev is arguably one of the more dangerous calculators around – and allowing the white pawn on b6 raised all sorts of red flags in my mind. I kept calculating and recalculating the lines to make sure that everything was fine – many more times than if the game hadn't been as crucial. As it turned out, White did have some brilliant tactics – which neither of us found, since they were a little too hard to find over the board.

34.b5 axb5 35.cxb5 ♖d5!

Continuing to play the forcing variations.

36.b6 ♖c3

37.♖e7?!

37.♘xd4!? would lead to some crazy lines if Black accepts the piece sacrifice, but he can at least play 37...♖xa5, which should be safe, since the b6-pawn will come under attack as well.

I was mostly worried when I calculated the crazy lines after 37.a6!!. I don't remember exactly what lines I saw – I certainly missed many things compared to the engines here – but my main aim was to convince myself that I wouldn't lose to some straightforward tactic, because my last few moves (taking the knight to a2, and bringing my rooks forward) would have looked particularly bad then: 37...bxa6 38.b7 (38.♘xd4 ♖c8, and everything seems extremely messy, but Black is at least hanging on) 38...♖b5 39.♘a5! ♖xb2 40.♖xd4 ♔g7

ANALYSIS DIAGRAM

I did consider this position in my calculations, but obviously did not see the amazing 41.♖d2! ♖xd2 42.b8♕. Now there are actually still decent chances to hold this position after 42...♖cc2 43.♕a7 ♖xf2 44.♕xf2 ♖xf2 45.♔xf2, so I guess entering the tactics was technically the right decision. But from a practical point of view, I needed to be more confident in my calculations and not check the lines so often.

37...♘b4!

Another move that took a lot of effort because of all the lines I tried to calculate – and here the calculations were already fairly easy. I could already sense that White might have gone wrong, but I did not quite trust myself yet, and spent a lot of time calculating lines that were obviously not good for White.

38.♖f3!?

After 38.♖xc3 dxc3 39.♘a4 c2 the pawn on c2 is far more dangerous than

the white pawns. For instance: 40.♖xb7 ♖xa5.

But all my calculations before 37...♘b4 were wasted when he immediately went for the text-move, a move I had not considered at all. Luckily, we were close enough to the 40th move, and not having too many options I went:

38...♖xf3 39.gxf3 ♘d7 40.♖e8+ ♔g7 Reaching move 40 was a huge relief, but the sequence of moves before this had taken its toll on me and I could feel my energy levels sagging.

41.♖c8 ♘c6!?

I wanted to continue in the same forcing way as in the last few moves, even though I no longer needed to. I should certainly have played a safe move like 41...♘a6. Here, I still had to calculate both a6 and ♖xc6 carefully – which I did. It wasn't too hard, but it did continue to wear me out.

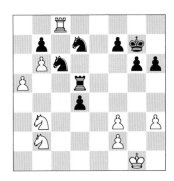

42.♖c7

This took me completely by surprise. After 42.♖xc6 bxc6 43.b7 Black can at least go 43...♖b5! 44.a6 ♖xb3! 45.a7 ♖xb7 46.a8♕ ♖xb2, and he is clearly not at risk.

The alternative 42.a6 ♖b5! looked messy, but it was fairly easy to calculate that things were OK for Black, since 43.♖xc6 bxc6 transposes to the 42.♖xc6 line we already saw.

42...♘xb6?

I continued to try and calculate lines, but here I completely missed White's reply. Instead of my mistake, 42...♖b5 was a fairly straightforward line that I just did not consider. It actually leads to crazy complications that I didn't even look at, thinking that 42...♘xb6 was probably enough to draw. If I had cal-

culated these lines, I think I would have seen that Black would probably be fine after 43.♘xd4 ♘xd4 44.♖xd7 ♘e2+. This leads to strange complications, but I think that practically speaking I need not have worried about the white pawns too much, since it feels as if the knight and rook would be able to hold.

43.♖xb7! ♘c8 44.♘c4!

Now the position is no longer easy for Black, and I was in no mental state to fight for a draw (1-0, 81).

You cannot always protect against tactical mishaps, but constantly worrying about them is not a solution either, as you saw above. Yes, there is a slightly higher risk that you may blunder if you are rusty, but this risk is always there. That is what makes chess exciting.

Conclusion

Playing after a long break does not mean you need to accept that you won't play as well as before. You need to find reasons to be excited about playing again. A few tips that may help you play better are:

■ Choose your openings carefully – especially try to avoid depending on your memory.

■ It is often easier to see attacking potential, especially for your opponent. Here, it is important to be aware of such tendencies, which can help you assess the position without bias and see the defensive potential.

■ Repeating calculations is obviously an apt strategy when rusty, but you have to realize that this also causes a lot of stress and tiredness. Thus, avoid doing this in most situations and be more confident in your calculations. ■

A Wing Gambit in the Symmetrical English

Jeroen Bosch

7.b4!?

'Its aim is to gain one lousy tempo to occupy the long diagonal in order to prevent Black from developing his kingside.'

This issue's Surprising Opening Secret is a wing gambit with a twist. Most wing gambits are played in order to gain influence in the centre. Consider, for example, 1.e4 c5 2.b4 (to lure the c-pawn away from square d4), or its stronger version against the French: 1.e4 e6 2.♘f3 d5 3.e5 c5 4.b4.

Alternatively, you may think of the Volga Gambit, in which Black sacrifices his queenside pawns for half-open files for his rooks.

Then there is the Evans Gambit (after 1.e4 e5 2.♘f3 ♘c6 3.♗c4 ♗c5), in which 4.b4 gains a tempo, so that after 4...♗xb4 5.c3 White can build up his centre (and use the a3-f8 diagonal).

The wing gambit that we will examine is fairly unique in that its aim is to gain one lousy tempo to occupy the long diagonal in order to prevent Black from developing his kingside. Are you interested? You should be!

1.c4 c5 2.♘f3 ♘f6 3.♘c3 d5

This line in the Symmetrical English is especially popular with Grünfeld players.

4.cxd5 ♘xd5 5.e3 e6

A solid line that may head towards a Semi-Tarrasch. Instead, 5...♘xc3 6.bxc3 g6 is in Grünfeld style, but recently 6.dxc3 has also come to the fore, games with which, e.g. Carlsen-Vachier-Lagrave (St. Louis 2017) and Radjabov-Svidler (Geneva 2017), have been analysed in this magazine.

6.♘xd5!?

This is already quite rare. Instead, it is common practice to go for an isolated pawn position with either 6.♗c4 ♘c6 7.0-0 ♗e7 8.d4 cxd4 9.exd4 0-0 10.♖e1, or 6.d4 ♘c6 7.♗d3 ♗e7 8.0-0 0-0 9.a3 cxd4 10.exd4.

Obviously, Black now has a choice as to how to take back on d5.

Variation I

6...♕xd5 Taking back with the queen avoids our wing gambit, but allows White to gain a tempo (b3 and ♗c4 will follow).

7.b3

7...♗e7 7...♘c6 8.♗c4 ♕f5 9.♗b2 e5?! (9...♗e7 transposes to Rakhmanov-Erdös, Linares 2017, see below), and now 10.d4! would have been pretty strong, while 10.g4!? was good fun (but no edge) after 10...♕g6 (10...♕xg4 11.♖g1 ♕f5 12.♘g5 ♗e7 is pretty unclear, and 10...♕f6 also has a right to exist) 11.h3 in Arribas-Sanchez, Mostoles 2013.

8.♗b2

Equally playable is 8.♗c4 ♕f5 9.♗b2 ♘c6 10.0-0 0-0 11.d4 ♖d8 12.♕e2 cxd4 13.♘xd4 ♘xd4 14.♗xd4, and here Black should be able to hold. However, in Rakhmanov-Erdös, Linares 2017, the solid Hungarian player failed to make it to a draw.

8...0-0 9.♗c4

Here is the tempo gain on the queen. White's advantage isn't all that large, but he runs no risk whatsoever, whereas Black will have to defend accurately. His first problem is where to move his queen?

9...♕d8 Withdrawing the queen is certainly the safest option. After 9...♕f5 10.♘e5! her majesty is suddenly in trouble: 10...♗d6 11.♗d3! ♕g5 12.f4, and the queen should finally have been withdrawn anyway.

For instance, 12...♕h4+ (instead, 12...♕h6? 13.♘g4 ♕h4+ 14.g3 ♕e7 15.♘f6+! was an outright win in Barsauskas-Roizman, Vilnius 1959) 13.g3 ♕e7, although 14.♕h5 f5 (14...g6 15.♕g4! e5 16.fxe5! ♗xg4 17.exd6 ♕xe3+ 18.dxe3 ♗xh5 19.♖c1 is great for White) 15.♘c4,

with g4 to follow, will make Black suffer as well.

Please note that because White hasn't castled yet, 9...♕h5 can be met by 10.g4!, and this is definitely good fun to play!

10.0-0 ♘c6 11.d4 cxd4 12.♘xd4

12...♘xd4 After 12...♗d7 White should not trade voluntarily with 13.♘xc6, since 13...♗xc6 14.♕g4 ♗f6 15.♖ad1 ♕e7 16.♗xf6 ♕xf6 yielded White nothing in Timman-Andersson, Wijk aan Zee 1979.
A serious option is maintaining the pressure with 13.♖c1, when 13...♖c8 is met by 14.♘b5!, and White is definitely better.
So Black should settle for 13...a6 14.♘f3!? or play 13...♘xd4 after all, when he would be very close to full equality after 14.♗xd4 ♗c6.
Therefore White should perhaps

avoid the knight trade altogether with 13.♘f3.

13.♗xd4 ♗f6 13...♗d7. **14.♕e2** Here 14.♗xf6 ♕xf6 15.♕d6 ♖d8 16.♕c7 may look annoying, but after 16...♖d7 17.♕g3 ♖d8! the position was equal in Pustovoitova-Ushenina, Novi Sad 2016.

14...♗xd4 15.♖ad1

15...♕e7 Black is still suffering a bit after 15...e5 16.exd4 exd4 17.♕e4 ♕f6 (17...♖e8? 18.♖xd4+−) 18.♕xd4.
16.♖xd4 16.exd4!? ♗d7 17.d5!? deserves attention. **16...e5** 16...♗d7!.
17.♖d2 a6 17...♗d7 18.♖fd1 ♗c6 19.♗b5!. **18.♖fd1 b5 19.♗d5** and Black still hadn't fully equalized in Gatterer-Votava, Austria 2016.

Variation II

6...exd5 Taking back with the pawn looks more solid, but it is exactly here that we have a cunning plan!

7.b4!?

An interesting wing gambit mainly designed to gain a necessary tempo needed to put pressure on Black's kingside. Black is facing the eternal problem: accept the gambit or not?

Variation IIa

Black refused the Greek gift in the stem game and went

7...c4

8.♗b2 ♗xb4 In case of something like 8...♘d7, White gets a comfortable edge for free: 9.a3 ♘f6 10.♗e2.

9.♗xg7 ♖g8 10.♗b2

This is how the inventor of 7.b4 continued. In the 2017 Tata Steel tournament, Nepomniachtchi, in his game against Harikrishna, went 10.♗e5!?, which aims to plant the bishop on g3 to protect the g-file and allow White to castle – this certainly makes sense! After 10...♘c6 11.♗g3 ♗f5 12.♗e2 ♗e7 13.0-0 it got messy with 13...h5! 14.d3 h4 15.♗f4

15...d4!? (15...b5!?) 16.exd4 ♘xd4 (16...♗h3 17.g3 ♗xf1 18.♗xf1 ♘xd4 19.♖b1, and Black is a full exchange up, although a powerful bishop pair and an exposed black king still point to an edge for White) 17.dxc4 ♘xe2+ 18.♕xe2 ♗d3?! (18...♕d3! 19.♕xd3 ♗xd3 20.♖fe1 ♗xc4 21.♖xh4 ♗e6 22.♘f3±) 19.♕e5 ♗xf1 20.♖xf1 ♖c8 21.♖e1 ♖c6 22.♘d4?! (22.♕h5!±) 22...♖cg6 23.g3 hxg3? (23...♔f8) 24.hxg3 ♔f8 25.♖d1 ♕d7 26.♖d2 ♖f6.

And here Nepo could have crowned his efforts with 27.♘f5! ♖xf5 (27...♕xf5 28.♗h6++−) 28.♗h6+ ♔e8 29.♕b8+, winning.

10...♘c6

It would be nice to keep the queen from reaching the b1-h7 diagonal, but 10...♗f5 fails to 11.♘d4 ♗g6 (11...♕d7 12.♘xf5 ♕xf5 13.a3 ♗a5 14.♕b1!?) 12.♕a4+, winning a piece.

11.♕c2

There is something to be said for 11.♕b1!? ♖g6 12.g3, when the bishop on b4 is 'hanging in the air' due to a future ♘f3-e5/d4.

11...♖g6

12.♗e2!?

There are plenty of alternatives that deserve attention at this stage, with 12.g3, 12.h4 and 12.♘e5 all springing to mind. White's position seems generally easier to play. It's unclear whether Black's king will find a safe haven.

12...♕e7 13.g3?!

13.h4! would have been quite annoying for Black.

13...♗h3! 14.♘h4

This was the plan, but Black can simply ignore the threat with:

14...0-0-0! 15.a3

Just as in the game, the roles would have been reversed after the immediate 15.♘xg6 fxg6. For a minor material investment, Black's king is brought to safety, while it is unclear where White's king will hide.

15...♗a5

16.♘xg6

Perhaps damage control with 16.♗f1!? was in order.

16...fxg6 17.♗c3 ♗b6 18.d4?! cxd3 19.♗xd3 ♔b8 20.0-0-0 ♖f8

Stronger than the text is 20...d4! 21.exd4, and now either 21...♗xd4 22.♗xd4 ♘xd4 23.♕b2 ♖d6 or 21...♗g4 22.♖de1 ♕xa3+ 23.♕b2 ♕f8, and in both cases it's easier being Black! Equally good is 20...♕xa3+ 21.♕b2 ♖d6.

21.♖d2 ♕xa3+ 22.♕b2 ♕e7 23.♔b1 ♗c5 with unclear play in Anton-Salem, Martuni 2015.

Variation IIb

7...cxb4

Black accepts the pawn on offer, but it will take some time before his extra pawn will count for anything. However, as Tarrasch already taught us: 'Before the endgame, the Gods have placed the middlegame'.

8.♗b2 ♘c6

Another idea is 8...♘d7 9.♖c1 ♘f6. Black wants to develop his kingside, but White now gains a positional edge by force: 10.♗b5+ (10.♗xf6 also works) 10...♗d7 11.♗xf6! gxf6 (11...♕xf6 12.♗xd7+ ♔xd7 13.♕a4+ ♔d8 14.♕a5+ wins on the spot)

12.♘d4 (12.♗xd7+ ♕xd7 13.♘d4) 12...♖c8?! 13.♗xd7+ ♕xd7 14.♖xc8+ ♕xc8 15.♕a4+ ♔d8 (15...♕d7 16.♕xa7) 16.0-0, and for only one pawn White gets a superior structure and a safe king, whereas Black's king will not find a safe spot to hide. 16...♗c5 17.♖b1!? ♗d6 18.♕d1 This was the point of 17.♖b1 – the rook is on the queenside and the queen will sow havoc on the kingside. 18...♗b8 19.g3 h5 20.♕f3 (20.♖c1) 20...♔e8 (20...♔e7 21.♘f5+ ♔f8 22.e4! dxe4 23.♕xe4+−) 21.♕xf6 ♖g8 22.♘f5 ♕f8 23.♕d4! ♖g6 24.♕xd5 ♖c6 25.♕e4+, and Black resigned, since all his weak pawns will drop off, Kuzubov-Schreiner, Hersonissos 2017.

9.♖c1!? White has great compensation for the pawn. The pressure along the long diagonal is tremendous. How is Black going to develop his kingside? He might play ...f7-f6, but this ugly pawn move creates clear weaknesses. Black, Dutch GM Benjamin Bok, in the end makes a few moves on the queenside first, only to play ...f7-f6 after all (on move 14).

9...a6 White is more comfortable after 9...f6 10.♘d4 ♘xd4 11.♗xd4 ♗e6 12.♗b5+ ♔f7 (12...♗d7? 13.♕h5+) 13.0-0.

10.♘d4

10...♘xd4!

The logical 10...♗d7 is met by the queen sortie 11.♕h5! ♘xd4 12.♗xd4 ♖c8 13.♖xc8 ♕xc8 14.♗e2, followed by castling (14.♕xd5? ♕c1+ 15.♔e2 ♗e7−+): 14...♗f5 15.0-0±. More subtle is 11...♖c8, planning 12.♕xd5?! ♘xd4! 13.♖xc8 ♗xc8 14.♕xd4 ♕xd4 15.♗xd4 ♗e6, and suddenly (after the trade of queens) the queenside pawns are more important than the central pawns. So after 11...♖c8 White should play 12.♘xc6 ♖xc6 (12...♗xc6 13.♗d3, and we might ask once more how Black is going to finish his development?) 13.♖xc6 bxc6! (13...♗xc6 14.♗d3) 14.♗xa6, and here Black could try the clever 14...h6!? (intending 15.0-0 ♕g5! 16.♕e2 ♗e7, and finally Black will be able to castle!). However, after 15.h4!?, which prevents ...♕g5, White should keep an edge.

11.♗xd4 ♗f5 12.♗e2

12...♕d7?!

This is a kind of half-move that does nothing to resolve Black's problems. Good or bad, it was time to think about developing the kingside. There are a couple of options available:
– Play the weakening 12...f6 now,

when Bok might have been worried about 13.♗g4, which explains 12...♕d7.
– Go for it with 12...♗d6!?, since 13.♗xg7?! ♖g8 14.♗d4 ♖xg2 is fine for Black. However, stronger is 13.g4! ♗e4 14.f3 ♗g6 15.♗xg7. Now 15...♕h4+ 16.♔f1 ♕h3+ 17.♔g1 ♖g8 18.♗d4 gives Black some dynamic chances for his inferior structure.
– Trade rooks with 12...♖c8 13.♖xc8 ♕xc8 14.0-0 before going 14...f6.

13.♕b3 Here 13.0-0 and 13.g4!? also make sense.

13...♗e6?! Once more, Black should have bitten the bullet with 13...f6.

14.0-0 f6

Finally. But Sargissian has gained sufficient time to claim an edge now with:

15.♗h5+! ♗f7 No good is 15...g6 16.♗xf6. **16.♗xf7+ ♔xf7?!** 16...♕xf7. **17.♗b6! ♗e7 18.♖c7 ♕d6 19.♖fc1**

White is in control of the only open file, and winning back the pawn is easy, while Black's king is still awkwardly placed.

19...♖he8 Taking the bishop is no option: 19...♕xb6? 20.♕xd5+ ♕e6 21.♖xe7+ ♔xe7 22.♖c7+. And White wins a pawn after 19...♖hd8 20.♖xb7 ♖d7 21.♗c5 ♖c8 22.♖xd7 ♕xd7 23.♕xb4.

20.♗a5!

Even stronger than 20.♖xb7 ♖ac8.

20...♖g8 21.♖xb7 ♖ac8 22.♖xc8 ♖xc8 23.g3 And now pawn b4 will fall as well. The game did not last much longer: **23...♖c4? 24.d3! ♖c3 25.♕a4 ♗f8 26.♗xb4** 26.♕e8. **26...♖c1+ 27.♔g2 ♕d8 28.♗xf8 ♕xf8 29.♕xa6** 1-0, Sargissian-Bok, Hersonissos 2017. ∎

Peter Svidler sets baffling record in Russian Championship

Youngsters wake up giant

In his home city of St. Petersburg, the amazing Peter Svidler won the Russian Championship for the eighth time, breaking Mikhail Botvinnik's record. The top seed had a sluggish start — while Fedoseev and Dubov set an inexorable pace — but once he started approaching the so-called 'Super-Final' as a training tournament and keeping himself from getting bored (as he put it), nothing could stop him. **VLADIMIR BARSKY** reports.

Peter Svidler, Russian Champion for the 8th time: 'I really like playing in

As part of the Chess in Museums program of the Russian Chess Federation, this year three Russian museums vied to be the venue of the 'Super-Finals' of the Russian championship. The Weapons Museum in Tula and the Yeltsin Centre in Yekaterinburg had good hopes to lure the country's best chess players to their city, but the winner was the Political History Museum in St. Petersburg, known to the people as the 'Kschessinska Mansion'. Matilde Kschessinskaya was a famous ballerina, a favourite of the last Russian Tsar Nikolai II. After Nikolai's abdication, Matilde escaped from the city, and her mansion was taken over by the Bolsheviks, headed by Lenin. That

was exactly 100 years ago, in the bloody year of 1917...

Kschessinskaya emigrated in good time from Russia, lived a long life, and left her memoirs. And now the mansion houses a very interesting museum, describing the grand and tragic history of our country in the 19th-21st centuries. The chess players played in two remote halls, amid a 'Women and the Revolution' exhibition. On the walls were numerous photographs and documents, and on the ceiling banners with texts such as 'Rise, women workers for the war against war!', or 'Women, remember that apart from the wash-tub and the stove there is also the school!'. After the tournament, over a friendly meal I asked the eight-times Russian champion Peter Svidler whether or

halls filled with the spirit of what came before us, rather than in a soulless room with walls the colour of stewed cabbage.'

not all this graphic campaigning had disturbed him.

'Generally speaking, in the hall there were tables that were better and those that were less good. There were boards where, when you were sitting at them, you didn't want to play chess, but to read what was written on the wall. When I played Evgeny Tomashevsky I was sitting alongside a letter by the grand duchess Yelena Serbskaya, devoted to what she and those close to her had endured during the storming of the Winter Palace. Displayed there were some extremely interesting historical documents. And on the other walls were displayed some completely fantastic texts about the personal lives of workers and peasants. "I will not go to the priest to marry my sweet tender friend, I will go to the commissar..." Of course, all this was a little distracting, but I really like playing in halls filled with the spirit of what came before us, rather than in a soulless room with walls the colour of stewed cabbage.'

Missing persons

The championships were held on the all-play-all system with 12 men and 12 women. The total prize fund for the two tournaments was 9 million roubles, which is about 125,000 euros. The male and female champions also each received a Renault Kaptur, a four-wheel drive city crossover.

Chess pessimists like to complain about the fact that tournaments are becoming fewer and fewer, and conditions for professionals – worse and worse. But is this so? For the moment I will say nothing about the championships in Saudi Arabia, and remind you that simultaneously with the Russian Championship there was the London Chess Classic, in which Sergey Karjakin and Ian Nepomniachtchi competed. During the same days Dmitry Jakovenko won the Russian Cup in Khanty-Mansiysk, while Alexander Grischuk, Alexandra Kosteniuk and Ekaterina Lagno went off to the Mind Games in China. Since we have begun talking about who was not in St. Petersburg, we should also remember Vladimir Kramnik, who for some reason no longer plays in the championship of the country. But even without these titled grandmasters there was a very strong and even field, with Peter Svidler and Valentina Gunina as the rating favourites (but the women's title was won by Aleksandria Goryachkina).

But the main heroes of the first four rounds were the young grandmasters Vladimir Fedoseev (born in 1995) and Daniil Dubov (1996), who between them chalked up 7½ points out of 8! Moreover, in brilliant style. They played easily and unrestrainedly, demonstrating a large reserve of fresh ideas. Thus a genuine adornment of the first round was Dubov's win over Sergey Volkov.

Volkov is famed for his deeply developed opening repertoire, but Daniil was able to surprise the highly-experienced grandmaster. True, Dubov stated at the press conference after the game that his opening preparation had concluded in the region of the 8th-9th moves, but it is not easy to believe this. A spectacular positional knight sacrifice enabled White to create a fearsome pawn phalanx in the centre, which literally 'stalemated' the black minor pieces.

Daniil Dubov
Sergey Volkov
St. Petersburg 2017 (1)
Slav Defence, Chebanenko Variation

1.d4 d5 2.c4 c6 3.♘f3 ♘f6 4.♘c3 a6 5.♕c2 b5 6.e4 dxc4 7.b3 ♕a5 8.♘d2 e5 9.dxe5 ♘g4 10.♗e2 ♘xe5 11.0-0 ♗e7 12.bxc4 ♗e6

13.♘d5! cxd5 14.cxd5 ♗d7 15.♗b2 f6 16.f4
With a very strong initiative.
16....♘c4 17.♘xc4 bxc4 18.♔h1 ♕a4 19.♕d2 ♗b4 20.♗c3 a5 21.e5 0-0 22.e6 ♖c8 23.a3

♗xc3 24.♕xc3 ♕b3 25.♕d4 c3 26.♖fb1 a4 27.♖xb3 axb3 28.exd7 ♘xd7 29.♗g4 b2 30.♖g1 ♖cb8 31.♗f5 ♖xa3 32.♗b1 ♖c8 33.♕b4 ♖a1 34.♕b7 ♖ca8 35.d6 g6 36.♕b3+
Black resigned.

Prizes for brilliancies

Not long before St. Petersburg, Dubov and Fedoseev had taken part in a tournament in memory of their contemporary and friend grandmaster Yury Eliseev (1996-2016). At the same time Dubov was also the chief organizer. The grounds for

playing were, of course, extremely sad, but the event was memorable for a curious feature: there were no prizes for the competitive results, only for brilliant play. Vladimir and Daniil created there a whole series of vivid games, and, as though by inertia, they continued acting in the same style in the main tournament of the year.

'For the moment I like the quality of my play, and not only the result', Vladimir Fedoseev admitted after his win in the second round. 'I was not planning at all to win this game, but from the very first moves a struggle developed. Then somewhere White afforded me a chance, and I was able to exploit it.'

Evgeny Tomashevsky
Vladimir Fedoseev
St. Petersburg 2017 (2)
Slow Slav

1.d4 d5 2.c4 c6 3.♘f3 ♘f6 4.e3 ♗f5 5.♘c3 a6 6.♗e2 h6 7.♘d3 ♗xd3 8.♕xd3 e6 9.0-0 ♗b4 10.♗d2 0-0 11.♖fd1 ♗a5

12.♖ab1 ♘bd7 13.b4 ♗c7 14.e4 ♘b6

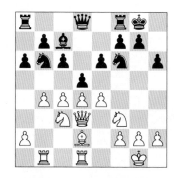

An ambitious move, which does not fit in very well with the words 'I was

not planning at all to win his game'...
15.cxd5 cxd5 16.e5 ♘fd7 17.♘e2 ♘c4 18.♘f4

Black's position looks very dangerous: it appears that his king will come under a crushing attack with sacrifices. But with two accurate moves Fedoseev not only eliminates all the threats, but also launches a counter-offensive.
18...♕e8! 19.♖e1 g5!
There were rumours that all this had been prepared in the home laboratory of Alexander Khalifman, who for many years has been training Fedoseev. It is hard to say whether

NOTES BY
Daniil Dubov

Peter Svidler
Daniil Dubov
St. Petersburg 2017 (2)
English Opening,
Symmetrical Variation

1.c4 g6!? Quite an ambitious choice, indicating that Black is ready to play both the Grünfeld (not an obvious choice against Peter) and sharp lines after 2.e4.

2.♘c3
This move made me feel optimistic. It took Peter more than 10 minutes to go for it. It's not that the move is bad in itself, but 2.e4 is far more dangerous.

2...c5 3.g3 ♗g7 4.♗g2 ♘c6 5.♘f3 d6 6.0-0

6...♗f5!?
Once again I decided to play the most ambitious line. Black has a pleasant choice here – for instance, both the sharp 6...e6 and the solid 6...e5 are perfectly playable.
6...♗f5 looks a bit dubious, but it's probably also a decent enough move.

7.h3
Otherwise Black would try to exchange the bishop on g2. For example, after 7.d3 ♕c8 8.♗d2 ♗h3 Black is fine.

7...♕c8 8.♔h2 ♘f6 9.d3 0-0 10.e4 ♗d7 11.♗e3
Now it looks as if White has a perfect version of the Closed Sicilian, but Black is still OK. No idea whether this can be explained – it's probably about chess being a drawish game.

Vladimir Fedoseev impressed with the depth and ingenuity of his opening preparation, which often suggested the hand of his trainer Alexander Khalifman.

this was indeed the case, but on the whole Fedoseev's opening preparation impressed with its depth and ingenuity. After Black's audacious move none of the sacrifices work, for example: 20.♘h5 f5 21.exf6 ♕xh5 22.♖xe6 ♘xf6 23.♖e7 ♗d6 etc. White is forced to sound the retreat.

20.♘e2 f6

21.♗c3!?
In the event of the exchange on f6, Black would have obtained a very favourable version of the French Defence, without the 'French' light-square bishop. Tomashevsky tried to complicate the play with the help of a

pawn sacrifice, but the compensation proved insufficient.

21...fxe5 22.♘xe5 ♘dxe5 23.dxe5 ♗xe5 24.♗xe5 ♘xe5 25.♕g3 ♘c4
And with accurate play Black converted his material advantage:

26.f4 ♕g6 27.♘d4 ♘d2 28.f5 exf5 29.♖bd1 ♘e4 30.♕e5 ♕f7 31.♘c2 d4 32.♖xd4 ♖ae8 33.♕d5 ♕xd5 34.♖xd5 f4 35.a3 ♔g7 36.♘d4 ♔g6 37.♘f3 ♘f6 38.♖d6 ♖xe1+ 39.♘xe1 ♖e8 40.♘d3 ♔f5 41.b5 a5 42.b6 ♖e7 White resigned.

'In the endgame I remembered Capablanca's words about the threat being stronger than the execution and, without trying to force events, I simply strengthened my position', Fedoseev related. And he promptly praised his rival, without forgetting, however, about himself: 'Danya has done well! Perhaps today I won a prettier game than him, but yesterday the day objectively belonged to him.'
The game he referred to was Dubov's win in the second round, with Black, against Peter Svidler.

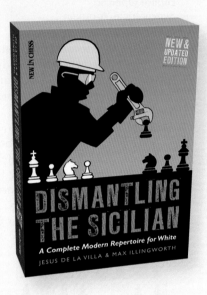
11...a6 12.♖c1 ♖b8 The first really important moment of the game.

13.♘d5 Obviously, we both started our calculations with the straightforward 13.d4, but after 13...cxd4 14.♘xd4 ♘xd4 15.♗xd4 ♕xc4! White has nothing, since after 16.♘d5

all the ambitions can be met by 16...♕xd4! 17.♕xd4 ♘g4+ 18.hxg4 ♗xd4, with a black edge.

Of course, after having seen the previous line, 13.b3 looks logical: 13...b5 14.cxb5 axb5 15.d4 cxd4 16.♘xd4 ♕a6. We both thought that this position was important. Peter told me after the game that in the end he decided that Black was better here. This is probably saying too much, but Black is definitely not worse. During the game I briefly calculated something like 17.♘d5 ♘xd5 18.exd5 ♘xd4 19.♗xd4 ♗xd4 20.♕xd4 ♖fc8, with equal chances. So it looks as if Black had managed to get a good position out of the opening.

13... ♕d8!
White had only two ideas: playing d4 at some point and ♘d5-b6xd7. The text-move prevents both.

14.b3 e6

15.♘c3 In the following amusing line: 15.♘xf6+ ♕xf6 16.♗g5, 16...♕b2! is the only move. And Black is probably even better here, since ...b5 is coming and White will never play d4.

15...e5
The position has become quite dry. Well, Black can try some expansion with ...b5, but White can either ignore it or prevent it with a4. In fact the only thing that can lead to a big fight here is one of the sides pushing his f-pawn. I considered it to be quite risky, and when Peter decided to do it, it was a pleasant surprise.

16.♘g1 ♘d4 17.♘ge2 b5 18.f4!?
As said, this doesn't look like a logical follow-up to me. Still, it's not a mistake yet.
A good alternative was 18.♕d2!?.

18...exf4

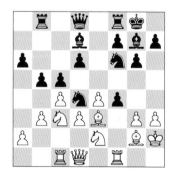

19.gxf4?! Objectively speaking, the first mistake of the game.
Peter thought that White would be worse after 19.♗xf4!? ♘xe2 20.♘xe2 ♗c6, but I failed to understand this after the game and I still don't: 21.♕d2 ♕c7 22.♗h6, with equality. The other option was 19.♘xf4!?.

19...b4! Now Black has a very simple

Daniil Dubov displayed great creativity and did not let himself be distracted by the 'Women and the Revolution' exhibition around him.

plan: he needs to push all White's pieces as far away as possible from the white king and then go for mate after ...♘h5 and ...f5.

20.♗xd4

It's funny that I was worried about 20.♘xd4?! cxd4 21.♗xd4 bxc3 22.♗xc3. I knew the computer would give Black a very large edge here, but from a practical point of view it didn't look that obvious to me. Now I've checked it and the engine gives around -2 with any normal move here. Still I think it was a good chance.

20...cxd4 21.♘b1 ♘h5

Besides a large advantage, Black has a very simple job.

22.♘d2 f5 23.c5!?

Peter decided that it was time for some kind of turnaround with some elements of bluff. And it was the move I was expecting.

23.exf5 ♗xf5 clearly favours Black.

23...dxc5 The most natural reply. Another line I calculated was 23...fxe4!? 24.c6 exd3 25.♘g3 ♗xc6 26.♖xc6 ♘xf4, and Black is attacking. Very tempting and probably suiting my style better; but I decided to take the pawn.

24.e5 That was his point: White has managed to keep the f-file closed and has some ideas with ♘c4-d6. Anyway, it's Black to move.

24...g5!?

And after this push White will be too late to defend everything.

25.♖xc5 ♕e7 26.♕c2

26.♖d5! was the last chance, although Black is clearly better after 26...♔h8.

26...♖bc8!?

I saw the cooperative line and decided to avoid it, although 26...♖fc8 was also good: 27.♗d5+ ♔h8 28.♖c1, and now Black should not play 28...♘xf4? (he is winning after 28...♗xe5!) 29.♖xc8+ ♖xc8 30.♕xc8+ ♗xc8 31.♖xc8+ ♗f8 32.♘xf4 gxf4 33.♘f3, with compensation for the material deficit.

27.♕c4+

This loses immediately, but the position is bad for White anyway.

He is lost after both 27.♖c1 ♘xf4 28.♘xf4 ♗xe5 or 27.♖xc8 ♖xc8 28.♘c4 ♘xf4 29.♘xf4 ♗xe5 30.♗b7 ♗xf4+ 31.♖xf4 ♕d6!.

27...♗e6 28.♕xe6+ ♕xe6 29.♗d5 ♖xc5 30.♗xe6+ ♔h8

31.♗c4 I was hoping for the following nice line: 31.♘f3 ♘xf4 32.♘xf4 ♗xe5! 33.♘xe5 ♖xe5, and Black wins.

31...♘xf4 White resigned.

■ ■ ■

It appeared that the tournament intrigue would reduce to a race between the young talents. I personally am very impressed by the fact that they are not obsessed only with playing, but they try themselves in various roles: organizers, trainers, commentators. Thus very recently on the outskirts of Moscow the Vladimir Fedoseev Chess Centre opened. Of course, the grandmaster does not sit there from morning until evening, but as far as he is

NOTES BY
Peter Svidler

Sergey Volkov
Peter Svidler
St Petersburg 2017 (3)
Grünfeld Indian Defence,
Russian Variation

I hadn't played Sergey Volkov for a long time, but in my preparation for this game I was pleased to see that not much has changed in the

'I decided that I would try in every game to do something which would be interesting for me myself.'

able he takes part in the work. And so, a fascinating Dubov-Fedoseev race was in prospect, but the young talents awakened Svidler...

A Hungry Svidler

A few years ago, somehow imperceptibly for myself, I became a fervent fan of Peter Svidler. And after his sluggish start (a short draw in Round 1, a loss in Round 2) I became pretty depressed. It was obvious that Peter was off his game. Of course, I thought, he would make an effort, somewhere he would use his class to win once or, with luck, twice and conclude the tournament decently, but nor more. But his next two games, I have to admit, staggered me – for a long time I hadn't seen such a hungry Svidler!

As Peter explained, the defeat against Dubov forced him to radically change his approach: 'I decided that I would play better if I were to regard the Super-Final as I would a training tournament. I would try in every game to do something, which would be interesting for me myself.'

In the third round it was 'interesting' for him to win a spectacular game with a piece sacrifice.

interim. As I mentioned in my notes to our previous encounter, way back in 2003 (see New In Chess 2003/7), my opponent is an extremely firm believer in his opening choices, to the extent that even I was able to correctly guess what to look at.

Another important thing to mention about this game is that it was played the day after I lost, deservedly, to Daniil Dubov as White. With Dubov and Fedoseev on an early lead and my own tournament off to as bad a start as I could remember, it was crucial to try to right the ship as soon as possible.

1.d4 ♘f6 2.c4 g6 3.♘c3 d5 4.♘f3 ♗g7 5.♕b3 Sergey has diversified a bit over the decades, but 5.♕b3 remains far and away his main weapon vs the Grünfeld.

5...dxc4 6.♕xc4

6...♗e6!?
Not a novelty as such, but this move is still relatively untried at GM level, compared to 6...0-0, or its spiritual brother, 4.♕b3 dxc4 5.♕xc4 ♗e6. Even 6...0-0 7.e4 ♗e6 has gained more traction so far.
The point of this is rather obvious – Black is planning to chase the queen to a place where it doesn't control the c5-break, and to do so at the earliest opportunity. It is also a very real pawn sacrifice, if White is so inclined.
7.♕a4+
7.♕b5+ ♗d7 8.♕xb7 ♘c6 is a mess. Sergey opted out of it pretty quickly, which I thought could mean either of two things: he was not very familiar with the rare line I had gone for, or he knew exactly what he was aiming for.
7...♗d7 8.♕b3
The game that first drew my attention to this line, Lysyi-Artemiev, Chita, Russian Championship 2015, went 8.♕c2 c5 9.d5 0-0 10.e4 e6, and Black got a very decent version of the usual 6...0-0 7.e4 ♘a6 lines.
8...c5 9.d5

All this was once again played very fast, and I sank into deep and somewhat dejected thought. Rare enough for me, I could remember exactly what my files said – but the prospect of those moves actually happening on the board filled me with dread. Having spent about 15 minutes looking for alternatives, and finding none that I liked, I braced myself and played:
9...b5
... only to be rewarded with an almost instantaneous:

10.e4

My files, which admittedly didn't deal with ♕b3/d5 in depth, said simply 10.♘xb5 ♕a5+ (in the interest of scientific integrity, I should mention that the immediate 10...♘a6, an idea that apparently eluded me entirely, is quite interesting here) 11.♘c3 ♘xd5 (11...♘a6, which I desperately tried to make work while deciding on 9...b5, fails to 12.♘d2! ♖b8 13.♘c4, and Black is nowhere near fast enough with his counterplay) 12.♕xd5 ♗xc3+ 13.♗d2 ♗xd2+ 14.♕xd2 ♘c6, with equality – both also totally devoid of winning chances.

As I mentioned, I haven't played against Sergey for a bit, or I wouldn't have worried nearly as much about those dry positions. 10.e4 was an immediate and much-needed reminder that my opponent, in his quiet way, is one of the most ambitious and combative players out there.

10...b4 11.e5 bxc3 12.exf6

12...♗xf6

A very typical (for me) decision. I chose not to spend almost any time at all on 12...cxb2 13.♗xb2 ♗xf6, instinctively preferring not to go for material over faster development.

Objectively, though, 12...cxb2 is quite strong: 14.♗xf6 exf6 15.♕e3+ ♔f8 16.♗c4 (16.♕xc5+ ♔g7 17.♗e2 ♖e8 is simply bad for White) 16...♕a5+ 17.♘d2 ♔g7, and only Black can be better, although White has decent chances to hold after 18.0-0 ♖e8 19.♘b3.

13.bxc3 0-0 14.♗h6

14...♖e8

I became briefly interested in 14...♗a4 15.♕a3 ♕xd5!? 16.♗xf8 ♕e4+ 17.♗e2 ♗b5, in particular the long line that went 18.0-0 (I failed to spot 18.c4 entirely, or I wouldn't have been nearly as excited by the whole thing: 18...♗xc4 19.♕e3 ♕xe3 20.fxe3 ♗xe2 21.♔xe2 ♗xa1 22.♖xe7 ♗g7 is just boring equality) 18...♗xe2 19.♖fe1 ♔xf8 20.♕b2 ♗xf3! 21.♖xe4 ♗xe4, with a very unusual position as the outcome. If Black gets his pieces out of the corner, he'll be much better, but I wasn't sure it was going to be all that easy after 22.♕b5!.

14...♕a5 15.♖c1 ♖d8 16.♘d2 is unclear as well.

15.♗c4

A very natural move – but I thought my reply would give me a very good game. I was more worried about the mess that was likely to happen after 15.♗e2: 15...♗a4 (if Black wants to avoid the forced lines, he could try 15...♕a5 16.♖c1 ♗f5 17.0-0 ♘d7 18.♘d2, but White is doing quite OK here) 16.♕xa4! ♗xc3+ 17.♘d2 (17.♔f1 ♗xa1 18.♗b5 ♖f8 is a clearly inferior version of the same) 17...♕xa1 18.♗b5 ♖f8 19.♗xf8 ♔xf8 20.0-0, and the extra pawn is not very keenly felt due to the pieces stuck in the corner.

A sample line could run 20...♗f6 21.♘b3 c4 (21...♕xd5? 22.♗e2!) 22.♕xc4 ♘d7, and Black is ever

Peter Svidler remembered the best advice his first trainer had given him: 'When they attack your pieces, make sure you actually *need* to defend them before you do.'

ETERI KUBLASHVILI

so slightly better, but a draw is an obvious favourite.

15...♗g4 16.♘d2 ♘d7

I had over-estimated this position quite a bit when playing 12...♗xf6. It's good for Black, but nowhere near as comfortable as I thought.

17.h3

White could start with 17.0-0, when Black has a choice between 17...♕a5 18.♖ac1 ♖ab8 19.♕c2 ♘e5 and 17...♖b8 18.♕a3 ♘b6 19.♗f4 ♘xc4 20.♘xc4 ♗e2 21.♗xb8 ♗xf1 22.♖xf1 ♕xb8 23.♘e3, with decent play in both cases.

Inserting 17.h3 makes a lot of sense – in many lines this will simply be a useful extra tempo.

17...♖b8

I decided I didn't need to allow 17...♗f5 18.g4 ♖b8 19.♕d1, when in fact after 19...e6! 20.d6 ♗xc3 21.♖c1 ♗b2 Black is seriously better. White would most likely play 18.0-0 anyway, after which the same choice between 18...♕a5 and 18...♖b8 – both sound options – would await me.

18.♕a3 ♗f5 19.0-0

19.g4?? ♘e5 20.gxf5 ♘xc4 21.♘xc4 ♕xd5 is no longer viable.

19...♘e5?!

My lifelong conviction that bishops must be preserved from being traded for knights played a trick on me here. I felt 19...♘b6 was too dry: 19...♘b6 20.♗b5 ♗d7 21.♘e2! (21.♗xd7 ♕xd7 22.♘e4 is also close to equality, although I preferred Black after 22...♗e5) 21...♘xd5 22.♘e4, and White is fine.

But I had completely missed Sergey's reply to 19...♘e5, and therefore didn't consider 19...♕c7 properly. Starting with this move makes a lot of sense – it strengthens both ...♘b6 and ...♘e5, and requires White to be very energetic if he's not to fall behind. However, making this move hinges on figuring out that 20.g4 is still not a threat because of the stunning 20...g5! 21.gxf5 ♕f4, and Black is better.

20.♗f4!

For some reason, I thought 20.♗b3 ♕c7 was forced, with a serious edge for Black.

20...♖b7

This decision took me a long time. After the first shock – 'but I can take your bishop, with my knight!' – had passed, I realized the position is now far from clear, and apart from the very obvious 20...♘xc4 21.♘xc4 ♗d3 22.♗xb8 ♕xb8 23.♘e3 ♗xf1 24.♖xf1, which is perfectly fine for Black, but also makes the position quite simple, and therefore a lot less attractive for my wounded '-1' mind-set, my options are rather limited. In the end, I opted for the text, hoping I had evaluated the complications after 21.♗a6 reasonably well.

21.♗xe5?!

Some people just don't value what they have. After 21.♗a6 ♖b6 22.♘c4 (22.♗xe5 ♗xe5 23.♘c4 ♗xc3! was what finally convinced me that 20...♖b7 was playable, but even here White is fine after 24.♕xc3 ♖xa6 25.♖fd1) 22...♗d3, White keeps things under control with 23.♗g3! (23.♘xb6? ♗xf4 is very good for Black) 23...♖xa6 24.♕xa6 ♕xd5 25.♘e3, even if after 25...♕e6 26.♕b5 ♖d8 27.♖ab1 h5 Black has enough for the exchange. The text-move is not horrible in itself, but Sergey connected it with an overly ambitious idea.

21...♗xe5

22.f4? It was not too late for 22.♗a6 ♖b8 23.♘c4, transferring the knight to e3 and coordinating the pieces, with near equality. But my opponent did not give up his dark-squared bishop to try to equalize.

After realizing that my opponent was planning to meet any bishop retreat with 23.g4 ♗d7 24.♘e4, followed by ♖ae1, ♕c1, f5 'and mate', I spent some time trying to solve that plan by peaceful means, and then remembered the best piece of advice my first coach had given me: 'When they attack your pieces, make sure you actually *need* to defend them before you do'. With that in mind, I began to look for ways to ignore 23.g4 when it came. To my delight, there turned out to be a lot of them, all of them seemingly playable. In the end, with 15 minutes left on my clock, I settled on:

22...♗d6

To my chagrin, the engines suggest that 22...♗c7!, which was an earlier discarded version of the same idea, is probably objectively stronger, since it gives White fewer bail-out options: 23.g4 (23.♖ae1 e5! 24.dxe6 ♗xe6 is quite bad for White as well – the fact that the knight on d2 is hanging is very relevant here) 23...e6! 24.gxf5 exd5 25.♗a6 ♖b6. During the game, I got to this position in my calculations, and then went looking for improvements, since it was not immediately clear to me just how overwhelming Black's obvious compensation due to White's disjointed pieces and ruined kingside really is. In fact, White is pretty much lost here.

23.g4

23...e6! I considered 23...e5 as well, but correctly decided that the position after 24.gxf5 ♕h4 25.♖f2! ♕g3+ 26.♖g2 ♕e3 27.♖f2 might not contain anything better than a perpetual.

24.gxf5

Perhaps Sergey did not realize in time just how bad his position would be if he accepted the sac and tried to hang on to the material. He could try 24.♘f3 here, although after 24...exd5 25.♗xd5 c4 26.♕a4 ♗c2! (a nice

thematic deflection shot I would need to find here) 27.♕xc2 ♗c5+ 28.♔h2 ♕xd5 his position would remain critical.

24...exd5

25.♗a6? The final mistake. He needed to find 25.♕a4!, keeping the queen tied to the d8-square by hitting the rook on e8. Black is still better after 25...♖b2! 26.fxg6 hxg6 27.♗xd5 (27.♖ad1 dxc4 28.♘xc4 ♖e4 loses) 27...♖xd2 28.♖ad1 ♖de2, but White is not entirely without hope here. 25.♗xd5? loses to 25...c4 26.♕a4 ♗c5+.

25...c4 26.♕a4 ♖b2

This is the position that convinced me that 22...♗d6 is stronger than 22...♗c7. With an additional tempo won by hitting the queen on a3, Black mounts an unstoppable attack against White's scattered forces.

27.♘f3 ♖ee2 28.♕c6

The easiest way to refute 28.♖ae1 turns out to be to trade some pieces: 28...♕b6+ 29.♔h1 ♖xe1! 30.♘xe1 ♕e3 31.♘f3 ♕e2, with mate.

28...♕e7

Sidestepping the threat of 29.♕c8. It's straightforward from here on in.

29.♕a8+

29...♗b8

An unnecessary finesse – 29...♔g7 30.♕xd5 (or 30.f6+ ♕xf6 31.♕xd5 ♗xf4, and it turns out White will never have enough time to play 32.♕d4) 30...♖g2+ 31.♔h1 ♕e2 would have won just as efficiently.

30.♕xd5 No good is 30.♖ae1 ♕e3+ 31.♔h1 ♕xf3+.

30...♗xf4 With the king on g8, White doesn't even have the illusion of the counterplay those lines with f6+ and ♕d4+ offered.

31.♖fe1

Played with seconds to spare. I had enough time here to figure out that 31...♖g5+ is a very pleasing bit of Black magic: 32.♘xg5 ♗e3+ 33.♔f1 ♖f2+ 34.♔g1 ♖g2+ 35.♔f1 ♖g1 mate, but decided it was too flashy. And anyway, the text-move finishes the game faster.

31...♕e3+ 32.♔h1 ♖h2+

And White resigned.

This game brought me back to 50% but, much more importantly, it gave me a much needed morale boost after the events of the previous round.

And after the next round the hope returned that Svidler could still fight for his eighth title.

Ernesto Inarkiev
Peter Svidler
St. Petersburg 2017 (4)
Four Knights Opening

1.e4 e5 2.♘f3 ♘c6 3.♘c3 ♘f6 4.♗b5 ♗d6 5.d3 h6 6.♘e2 a6 7.♗a4 b5 8.♗b3 ♘a5 9.d4 ♘xb3 10.axb3 ♘xe4 11.dxe5 ♗c5 12.♕d5 ♗xf2+ 13.♔f1 ♗b7 14.♕xb7 c6 15.♘ed4

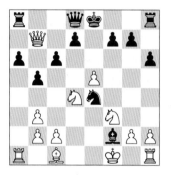

Here Black could have regained the piece – 15...♗xd4 16.♘xd4 ♘c5 17.♘xc6 ♗xb7 18.♘xd8 ♘xd8 with a probable draw. Instead of this there followed:
15...0-0!? 16.b4 f5 17.c3 ♗xd4 18.cxd4 ♕e7 19.♔e2 ♕xb4
The game also ended in a draw, but after wild complications.

'If I had thought that the draw was altogether no problem, I would probably have played it', said Peter, in answer to my question as to why he did not go into the ending. And he promptly added: 'Although, to be honest, I am not sure about that. Even after defeating Volkov the day before, I was only on fifty percent, whereas by that time other players had already won a mass of games, and I thought that I was not especially participating in the race, but solving my inner problems. The chief of these was that I was making every effort that I should not to be bored. Because when I become bored, I play

worse. And I was very happy when I found an opportunity to create chaos.

'Furthermore – when Ernesto and I gave an interview after the game, we both said that the computer would almost certainly refute this idea, but it was interesting to test it in a practical game. And on verification it transpired that, until I began playing obvious rubbish in time-trouble, up to that point the game was of quite decent quality. And the decisions which seemed good to me, were in fact good. Of course, the computer makes other moves, but it does not verbally abuse my moves. This was also pleasant. When you play such a complicated game, and later the impartial judge says: "Yes, in content this was not a catastrophe", this is a psychological support.'

In the 5th round Peter Svidler won an excellent game against Evgeny Romanov, reached +1, and, as they say, rejoined the battle. But in the middle of the tournament the young players, by contrast, slowed down. The first to stumble was Dubov: in the same 5th round he lost to Tomashevsky, after which he commented very sceptically on his play: 'I played like an idiot.' And Fedoseev lost two games in a row – in Rounds 6 and 7.

Vladimir Fedoseev
Vladimir Malakhov
St. Petersburg 2017 (6)
Slav Defence

Vladimir Malakhov has been operating at this level for many years, and after **1.d4 d5 2.c4 c6 3.♘f3 ♘f6 4.♘c3** he invariably plays the Chebanenko system, i.e. 4...a6.
But here there suddenly followed:
4...dxc4!?
It turned out that the one to 'blame' was his trainer Zvjaginsev, cunning Vadim, who on the free day had forced his pupil – to read a book! And not some book of Pushkin's stories, but Konstantin Sakaev's monograph on the Slav Defence.

As a result, the home preparation of Fedoseev/Khalifman was avoided. However, the leader did not aim to consolidate and he went in for one of the critical lines. Only, Fedoseev began working at the board from move 5, whereas Malakhov 'brought from home' as many as 23. An enormous handicap! In a position where accuracy was demanded of Black to maintain the balance, Fedoseev got carried away and allowed a pretty stroke.

position after 29.♗e2

At an appropriate moment White wanted to advance his pawn to h6, so for several moves he had avoided the exchange on g6. But as a result he simply lost it:
29...♕xh5!! 30.♕xd3 ♕xh1

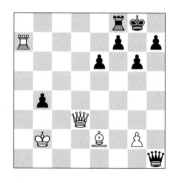

And White's position became difficult.

After this Fedoseev somehow feebly lost to Nikita Vitiugov, and the tournament situation became intricate in the extreme: the race was led by Fedoseev, Dubov and Vitiugov with 4½ out of 7, with Svidler and Tomashevsky half a point behind. The next day the meeting of the two leaders of the young generation of Russian players took place. Fedoseev gained an overwhelming advantage in Dubov's variation of the Grünfeld Defence (the line 1.d4 ♘f6 2.c4 g6 3.♘c3 d5 4.♗g5 c5!? should rightly bear Dubov's name), but then the miracles began.

Vladimir Fedoseev
Daniil Dubov
St. Petersburg 2017 (8)

position after 32...♖b4

'I was sitting and cursing, when suddenly my opponent surprised me', Dubov admitted after the game. 'He had masses of time, around 30 minutes, but almost without thinking he made an outwardly pretty, but, as it seemed to me, not very accurate move.

33.♘e7?! 'This was simply a nervy decision', Fedoseev ascertained. 'It is irresponsible to play like this. After all, I did not even calculate the variations; I simply saw a pretty move – and I made it.'

A little clarification: Dubov was cursing, naturally, mentally, and not aloud. Black's only hope was his passed c3-pawn; after the accurate 33.♘f4 the knight would have returned to the defence, and Black would soon have had to admit defeat. Playing for outward effects cost White dearly.

33...♖b5 34.♘g8 c2 35.♘xf6+ ♔e7 36.♘d7 ♖a8 37.h4 ♖a1 38.♔e2 ♔xe6 39.♘f8+ ♔f7 40.♔d3 ♖d5+ 41.♔xc2 ♖a2+ 42.♔c3 ♖xf2 43.♘e6 ♖xg2

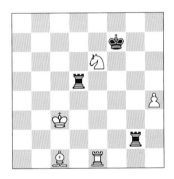

Very little material is left on the board, and in addition White has not managed to coordinate his pieces.

44.♘g5+ ♔g6 45.♖h1 ♖c5+ 46.♔d3 ♖g3+ 47.♗e3 ♖a5 48.h5+ ♔f5 49.♘e4 ♖a3+ 50.♘c3
Draw.

But the main miracle of the Super-Final occurred in the penultimate round.

Vladimir Fedoseev
Peter Svidler
St. Petersburg 2017 (10)
'Because of the rule which forbids offering a draw before the 40th move,

Nikita Vitiugov's risky attempt to correct the loss in the first tiebreak game has backfired. After 18 moves he stops the clock and is the first to congratulate Peter Svidler.

I have probably already lost 70 rating points!', Fedoseev lamented heatedly after the game.

'Yes, it's a long time since I was so lucky!', Svidler admitted. 'Volodya is a very ambitious player, but here this trait let him down: he made a couple more moves "for a win" than he should have done.'

position after 35...f6

36.♖c6 fxg5 37.f5? gxf5 38.exf5 ♔f8 39.♖h6 ♖c7 40.♗e4
Why did White sacrifice a pawn? According to Svidler, the only way for Black to lose was to blunder into a fork. On realizing his mistake, at this moment Fedoseev offered a draw.

'But, with 5 seconds on my clock, I found the strength to play on,' said Svidler. 'After all, I am a pawn up, and this was the first time I had stood so well in this game.'
However, the position remains a draw, but accuracy is required of White.
40...♖c4 41.♗g2 e4 42.♖f6+ ♔g7 43.♖g6+ ♔f7 44.♖xg5 ♖c1+ 45.♔f2 ♖c2+ 46.♔g1 ♖c1+ 47.♔f2 ♖c2+ 48.♔g1 e3 49.♗f3 ♖c1+ 50.♔g2 ♖c2+ 51.♔g1 ♖f2 52.♗xh5+ ♔f6 53.♖g4 ♖c2 54.♖d4 ♗c4 55.♖d1 ♔g5 56.♗f3 ♖f2 57.♗g2 e2 58.♖e1 ♖xf5 59.♗h3 ♖f3 60.♗g2 ♖f8 61.♗h3 ♗d3 62.♖a1 ♗c4

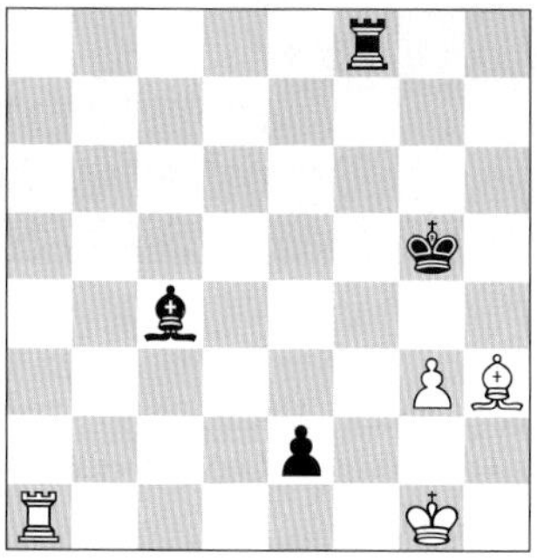

Of course, Fedoseev could have given up bishop for pawn and obtained the notorious endgame 'rook against rook and bishop'. but no one likes defending it for 50 moves. In the end Vladimir found a drawing set-up – and destroyed it with his own hands!
63.♖a5+?? ♔f6 64.♖a1
White was obviously counting on 64.♖f5+ ♔e7 65.♔f2, but then he noticed 64...♔g6!. The impulsive rook check allowed the black king to break through in the centre, and White's position became hopeless.
64...♔e5 65.g4 ♔d4 66.g5 ♔c3 67.♔h2 ♔d2 68.♔g3 e1♕+ 69.♖xe1 ♔xe1 70.♗g4 ♗d3
White resigned.

Inspired by this present, Svidler also won in the last round.

'I think that I conducted the game with Malakhov very decently. To defeat such a high-class, correct player as Volodya by nuances is always a pleasant feeling. Because with me, to be honest, this does not happen regularly!'

Vitiugov also won and reached +3. But Fedoseev missed quite good winning chances, finished on +2, shared 3rd-4th places with Dubov, and on the tie-break coefficient ended up outside of the prize list.

According to the rules, the fate of first place was decided in a rapid-play tie-break. Svidler had this to say: 'Nikita and I were incredibly tired, of course. In the first game I gradually equalized, and then I looked: I had equalized so well that I could continue playing for a win! Well, and Nikita made the last mistake.'

In the second game it was sufficient for Svidler to make a draw with White. In trying to complicate the play, Vitiugov began avoiding exchanges and simplification, but he quickly overstepped the boundary of acceptable risk. As early as the 18th move Nikita admitted defeat.

'I tried hard, I fought, but even so the tournament would have been won by someone else, had it not been for the miracle in the game with Fedoseev', Peter Svidler summed up his performance. 'In that game to a large extent I was a spectator, observing from the stalls what was happening. Unexpectedly Fedoseev offered me a chance, which I was obliged to exploit. Of course, I very much wanted to win the championship for the eighth time – this motivated me.

'In my native St. Petersburg it is a long time since any major chess events were held, and I realized that it would not be easy, because for me playing at home is more of a burden than a relief. On the other hand, it is good that a tournament takes place at home. I am not such an egoist, as to think only about what is good for me personally. St. Petersburg undoubtedly needs big tournaments, and it is bad that there have not been any for so long.'

'For me playing at home is more of a burden than a relief.'

Peter Svidler has surpassed the record of the great Mikhail Botvinnik – he has now won the championship of the country for the eighth time. Bravo! And it is especially pleasant that in this tournament he demonstrated such sparkling, confrontational play! ■

St. Petersburg 2017

					1	2	3	4	5	6	7	8	9	10	11	12		TPR
1	Peter Svidler	IGM	RUS	2763	*	½	0	1	½	½	1	½	½	½	1	1	7	2774
2	Nikita Vitiugov	IGM	RUS	2721	½	*	½	1	½	½	½	½	½	½	1	1	7	2778
3	Daniil Dubov	IGM	RUS	2677	1	½	*	½	0	½	0	1	½	½	1	1	6½	2752
4	Vladimir Fedoseev	IGM	RUS	2718	0	0	½	*	1	1	0	½	1	1	½	1	6½	2748
5	Evgeny Tomashevsky	IGM	RUS	2702	½	½	1	0	*	½	½	½	½	½	½	1	6	2714
6	Alexander Riazantsev	IGM	RUS	2651	½	½	½	0	½	*	½	½	1	½	½	1	6	2718
7	Vladimir Malakhov	IGM	RUS	2690	0	½	1	1	½	½	*	½	0	½	½	1	6	2715
8	Ernesto Inarkiev	IGM	RUS	2683	½	½	0	½	½	½	½	*	½	½	½	½	5	2663
9	Sanan Sjugirov	IGM	RUS	2650	½	½	½	0	½	0	1	½	*	½	1	0	5	2664
10	Maxim Matlakov	IGM	RUS	2738	½	½	½	0	½	½	½	½	½	*	½	0	4½	2631
11	Evgeny Romanov	IGM	RUS	2626	0	0	0	½	½	½	½	½	0	½	*	½	3½	2555
12	Sergey Volkov	IGM	RUS	2649	0	0	0	0	0	0	0	½	1	1	½	*	3	2532

WESLEY SO

presents:

My Black Secrets in the Modern Italian

and

My Secret Weapon: 1.b3

MY BLACK SECRETS IN THE MODERN ITALIAN

The Italian Game is considered a sound but quiet opening without early trades, giving rise to rich positions where plans are more important than forced variations — in short, an ideal avenue to outplay your opponent without having to learn much theory. But how should you approach new positions and keep a clear head in view of so many playable possibilities? The best way is this: you sit down next to a world class grandmaster and just listen to him!

In a total of nine video clips, top ten player Wesley So talks to IM Oliver Reeh, explaining his personal preferences as Black in the Italian game. The videos are structured according to specific concepts and ideas. Should Black play ...a6 to allow the retreat ...Ba7 or rather ...a5? What's the best way to meet White's plan with Bg5, be it with or without short castling? When is it possible to unleash the early raid ...Ng4 followed by ...f5? What are benefits of the knight manoeuvre Nc6-e7-g6 combined with Nf6-h5? Can one do without ...d6 and play ...d5 rightaway to sharpen up the game immediately? These and many more features the grandmaster explains for Black, providing his White perspective too - as a top gun, So of course employs the Italian with both colours!

Plans, tricks and subtleties in the Italian Game, well-structured and conceptual, explained by a world-class grandmaster — this DVD can take you towards the very top!

MY SECRET WEAPON: 1.b3

The Nimzowitsch-Larsen Attack with 1.b3 (or 1.Nf3 followed by 2.b3) is a system, rather neglected by theorists, which nevertheless can be a forceful weapon in the hands of an ambitious white player. Even Bobby Fischer tried this opening in various games, sometimes preferring it to his beloved 1.e4, and its greatest advocate was the legendary Danish fighter Bent Larsen. Meanwhile, 1.b3 has also found its way into the practice of today's world elite, and now finally a modern top ten player has taken on the subject for ChessBase: none other than Grandmaster Wesley So!

In a total of nine video clips, So talks to IM Oliver Reeh, explaining his view of White's strategy after the four main replies by Black: 1...e5, 1...d5 (2.Nf3!), 1...c5 and 1...Nf6. Often, play transposes to openings like the Queen's Indian or the Nimzo Indian with reversed colours where White simply is a valuable tempo up. Also possible are transitions to the English where once again the move 1.b3 proves very advantageous to White — his bishop will always be the first to appear on the long diagonal!

This DVD also provides insights in the personal thinking of a modern top grandmaster. For example, you'll get to know that So particularly appreciates the bishop pair, but also enjoys enemy doubled pawns (after for instance, Bb2xNf6!). Broaden your chess mind with GM Wesley So and 1.b3!

34,90 €   **34,90 €**

ChessBase GmbH · News: en.chessbase.com · CB Shop: shop.chessbase.com
CHESSBASE DEALER: NEW IN CHESS · P.O. Box 1093 · NL-1810 KB Alkmaar
phone (+31)72 5127137 · fax (+31)72 5158234 · WWW.NEWINCHESS.COM

You don't have to take back

The inverted 'en passant' is an option well worth keeping in mind. If it works, it's bound to throw your opponent off balance.

Your opponent is going to exchange off a pair of pawns, he thinks; but instead of mechanically taking back his pawn, you go for a pawn thrust aiming for active and aggressive play. 'En passant', but the other way around! Here's a fine example to demonstrate the concept.

Alexey Shirov
Richard Rapport
Baku Olympiad 2016
Ruy Lopez, Neo-Steinitz Variation

1.e4 e5 2.♘f3 ♞c6 3.♗b5 a6 4.♗a4 ♞ge7 5.c3 d6 6.d4 ♗d7 7.h4 Typical Shirov? Actually, it was Euwe who introduced the move in this position against Reshevsky in the World Championship Tournament in 1948 (having tried 7.♗b3 against Keres in the first round) – quite a logical positional move, in fact, in view of Black's further development options of ...g7-g6 or ...♞e7-g6. **7...h6 8.h5 ♞g8** Larsen specialized in this line for Black at some stage, and he reckoned the only way out for Black was capturing on d4. After 8...exd4 9.♞xd4 ♞xd4 10.cxd4 d5 he won a good game against Quinteros (Manila 1973). **9.d5 ♞ce7 10.c4 b5 11.♗c2 f5 12.♞h4 f4 13.g3**

13...fxg3 14.f4!? Go! No recapture, but this breaking move was White's plan when he played 13.g3. Shirov takes a direct shot

at Black's central pawn chain. Black's king in the middle and his hampered pieces are a clear incentive to try and open up the position. **14...♞f6** After 14...exf4 15.♗xf4 ♞f6 16.♗xg3 ♗g4 17.♕d4 ♗xh5 18.♞c3 White's spatial advantage gives ample compensation. **15.fxe5 ♗g4 16.♕d3 ♞xh5** Complicating the position. After 16...dxe5 17.♕xg3 ♗xh5 18.♞c3 ♕d6 19.♞f3 White has a smooth game. **17.e6**

17...♞g6? A miscalculation. No solution either was 17...g2 18.♞xg2 ♞g6 19.♖xh5 ♗xh5 20.♕h3, so 17...c6 seems to be the only move, but after 18.♗e3 or 18.♞c3 White is still pressing, partly thanks to his by now impressive central pawns. **18.♞xg6 ♕f6 19.♕f1!** A surprise, and the most convincing refutation. **19...♗f3** Because 19...♕xg6 fails to 20.e5!. **20.♖g1 ♗e7 21.♞xh8 ♕d4 22.♖g2** Black resigned.

Here there certainly was some fire on the board, but you can encounter similar pawn thrusts in various other openings – and in games from all times.

Efim Bogoljubow
Alexander Alekhine
Germany Wch Match 1934 (21)
Queen's Gambit Declined

1.d4 d5 2.♞f3 e6 3.c4 a6 Not a very common move, but at the time also practised by Alekhine's contemporaries Rubinstein and Euwe – and these days by the likes of Mamedyarov and Carlsen. **4.c5 b6** 4...♞c6 5.♗f4 ♞ge7 6.♞c3 ♞g6 7.♗e3 b6 8.cxb6 cxb6 9.h4 was the famous game Alekhine-Rubinstein, The Hague 1921 (1-0, 50). **5.cxb6**

5...c5!? Reckoning that the b6-pawn can be regained later anyway, Black immediately takes a shot at the centre. **6.♞c3 ♞d7** 6...cxd4 seems the correct and consistent follow-up, not fearing the materialistic 7.♞a4, when Black can continue to develop with 7...♞f6, enjoying the centre and trusting to win back b6 in due time. **7.♞a4 c4?** A strange and illogical decision, where again 7...cxd4 would be appropriate. Alekhine was clearly worse after **8.♗d2 ♗d6 9.b3 ♗b7 10.e3**

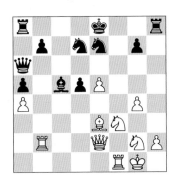

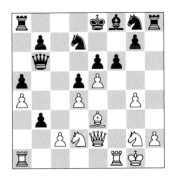

and eventually only managed to take the game after a peculiar blunder by Bogoljubow (0-1, 63).

In the following game, Black's seemingly solid pawn chain was annihilated surprisingly quickly. The way this happened will begin to look familiar to you.

Milos Perunovic
Bojan Vuckovic
Vrnjacka Banja 2010
Caro-Kann, Advance Variation

1.e4 c6 2.d4 d5 3.e5 ♗f5 4.♘d2 e6 5.g4 ♗g6 6.♘e2 ♕b6 7.♘b3 ♘d7 8.♗e3 h5 9.♘f4 ♗e4 10.f3 ♗h7 11.♕e2 hxg4 12.fxg4 a5 13.a4 ♗e4 14.♗g2 ♗xg2 15.♘xg2 c5 16.0-0 c4 17.♘d2 f6
White has established a pleasant lead

21.dxe5 ♗c5 22.♖ab1 Only now does White pay attention to the b3-pawn. **22...b2 23.♘f3 ♘e7 24.♖xb2 ♕a6**

25.e6!? An original thought, opening the e-file by sacrificing this pawn. **25...♕xe6 26.♘g5 ♕e5 27.♘f3 ♕e6 28.♗xc5 ♕xe2 29.♖xe2**

'Another typical case of a pattern you can only detect if you have switched off your auto-pilot.'

in development and now sensed that it was time to break open the position to optimally exploit the black king's vulnerable position. **18.b3** This apparently innocent nibbling at Black's pawn chain was obviously meant to meet **18...cxb3**

... with the energetic **19.c4!? fxe5 20.cxd5 exd5** Since 20...exd4 21.♘c4 ♕c5 22.♘f4 (22.dxe6 ♘e5) 22...dxe3 23.♘xe6 ♕b4 24.♕xe3 probably didn't appeal to Black. White has a draw by repetition in hand and can try for more, while 24...♕xc4 is refuted by 25.♘xg7+ ♔d8 26.♘e6+ ♔e8 27.♖f4.

♘xc5 **30.♘g5** Even with the queens off, the pinned knight and the undeveloped black rooks make life difficult for Black. **30...b6 31.♖f7 ♘e4?** 31...♖a7 was the only move. **32.♖xg7 ♘xg5 33.♖exe7+ ♔f8 34.h4 ♘f3+ 35.♔f2 ♘xh4 36.♘f4 ♖h6 37.♖ef7+ ♔e8 38.♘xd5 ♖c8 39.♘f6+ ♖xf6+ 40.♖xf6** Black resigned.

Now witness the same break, this time in the centre, in a middlegame in which the queens have already been exchanged.

Richard Rapport
Matthieu Cornette
Karlsruhe 2016
English Opening

1.g3 e5 2.c4 c6 3.♘f3 e4 4.♘d4 d5 5.d3 ♗b4+ 6.♗d2 ♕b6 7.♗xb4 ♕xb4+ 8.♕d2 ♕xd2+ 9.♘xd2 exd3 10.e4! Two squares ahead, past the capturing pawn again, and the most straightforward way to seize the centre. And a novelty. Here, only the more cautious 10.e3 had been tried in Benko-Zuidema, in Belgrade in 1964.

10...dxe4 A logical reply, since it removes White's central pawn. Not the best, though. Apart from the fact that the knight will now eye d6, the black king will be exposed on the open e-file, even though the queens have already been exchanged. After the other capture, 10...dxc4 11.♘xc4, the white knight also annoyingly aims for d6. Thus, a developing knight move seems better, although White keeps an edge after 10...♘f6 11.cxd5 cxd5 12.e5 ♘g4 13.f4 or 10...♘e7 11.cxd5 cxd5 12.♘b5. **11.♘xe4 ♗e7 12.0-0-0 ♘f6 13.♘c5!?** 13.♘xd3 is the most obvious continuation, but after 13...♖d8 Black may well get away with his lag in development. **13...g6?** Too slow, but after 13...♖d8 14.♖xd3 ♘bd7 Black may have feared the unpleasant 15.♖e3+. **14.♗g2 ♘bd7 15.♖he1+ ♔f8 16.♘xd3**

Now White had a huge lead in development and Rapport patiently hauled in the point (1-0, 34).

This inverted 'en passant', a sacrifice and a break at the same time, is another typical case of a pattern you can only detect if you have switched off your auto-pilot and do not recapture automatically. Let's hope the above examples have stored this pattern in your memory or subconscious. ∎

Judit Polgar

Adjournments, anyone?

They were abolished not that long ago, but for many young players the phrase 'adjourned games' barely rings a bell. Yet, **JUDIT POLGAR** argues that this now obsolete phenomenon is a good reason to study the classics.

Even though the rules of how to move the pieces have stayed unchanged for half a millennium, a series of off-board rule modifications have been made over the last few decades that have had a heavy impact on tournament life. One of the most important changes was the elimination of adjournments. These days, a game is finished in one session, whereas not that long ago games could be interrupted (adjourned) after a certain number of moves (or hours of play), to be resumed later that day or even the next day.

My feeling is that the younger generation consider the adjournment system as mysterious and archaic as the dial-disc telephone. Therefore I will highlight some of the basic aspects of it, while showing you some telling examples.

For many decades, adjourned games were a strong stimulant for the development of endgame theory. Chess players are especially effective in analysis when under pressure, and there was an abundance of pressure when facing the resumption of the game later that evening, the next morning or, in certain elite tournaments, on an otherwise free day reserved for adjourned games.

Here is a classic example that brought about a radical change in the assessment of an important type of endgame.

Mikhail Botvinnik
Nikolay Minev
Amsterdam Olympiad 1954

position after 72...♕c8+

Ten years earlier, Botvinnik had won a similar endgame against Ravinsky in the Soviet Championship, but in the meantime Keres had published an article recommending a defensive system based on keeping the king on a4 or a5. While analysing alone (quite an unusual situation during Olympiads!) until deep into the night, Botvinnik delved into the essence of the position. White should not try to support his pawn with the king, as in

rook endings, but use his king to attack his rival instead! After this revelation winning proved a mere formality:
73.♔g5 ♕d8+ 74.♕f6 ♕d5+ 75.♕f5 ♕d8+ 76.♔h5 ♕e8 77.♕f4+ ♔a5 78.♕d2+ ♔a4 79.♕d4+ ♔a5 80.♔g5 ♕e7+ 81.♔f5 ♕f8+ 82.♔e4 ♕h6 83.♕e5+ ♔a4 84.g7 ♕h1+ 85.♔d4 ♕d1+ 86.♔c5 ♕c1+ 87.♔d6 ♕d2+ 88.♔e6 ♕a2+ 89.♕d5 ♕e2+ 90.♔d6 ♕h2+ 91.♔c5

White is ready to meet any new check with a countercheck, so Black resigned.

Many such endgame secrets have been discovered by great players during their nightly analysis. For less experienced players, adjournments used to be helpful from a learning point of view. The wise ones would never go to a tournament without a good endgame book for checking and learning the theory related to the adjourned position they had reached. I clearly remember such an example from my own practice.

Judit Polgar
Gudmundur Gislason
Reykjavik 1988

position after 82...♔b7

The game had been adjourned for the first time after move 69. Things went well for me, for I had reached a theoretically winning ending. I was sure about the evaluation and even remembered the draft plan. But because I didn't want to mix things up, I decided to mark time until the game would be adjourned again to recheck the theory.

With hindsight, I am a bit surprised by this wise attitude, because I was

103.♖b7+ ♚c8 104.♖b5 ♗f2

104...♚c7 is a better defence, with the main line going: 105.♖b3 ♗f2 106.♖c3+ ♚b8 107.♖f3 ♗g1 108.♖b3+ ♚c7 109.♖b7+ ♚c8 110.♖b5!! ♚c7 111.♚a5, followed by ♚b4.

105.♚a5!

My opponent must have been aware of the winning plan as well, because after seeing this crucial move he immediately resigned. Play might have continued: 105...♗e1+ 106.♚b6 ♚b8 (if

At this point, the time allocated to the playing session had run out, and the arbiter approached our board with the envelope in his hand, a clear sign that the game had to be adjourned. My opponent must have felt my lack of confidence in this endgame, because he flashed out the tricky:

81.♚e4

Practically forcing me to seal the move at a point when a crucial decision was required.

81...♚h4?!

This is not the losing move yet, but it turns a comfortable drawn position into one which is extremely difficult to defend correctly over the board.

I knew that after White's king's move there is one optimal black king move, but could not remember to which side. In fact, 81...♚h6! is considered the best reply, preventing White from building up any constructive plan.

After the adjournment I had analysed the endgame with my sister Susan, but the course of the game shows that with limited time I could not assimilate all the ideas properly. Unfortunately, my opponent was aware of the winning ideas.

82.♖g1 ♚h5 83.♗f7+ ♚h6 84.♚f4

'For the young generation the adjourning system is something as mysterious and archaic as the dial-disc telephone.'

very impatient when I was 11, which caused me to spoil many good positions or come close to doing so by hurried decisions. After move 100, we reached the following position.

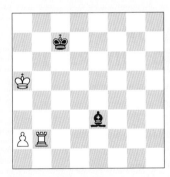

And the long-awaited second adjournment. As you can see, I had played super-safely (I knew I could have advanced the pawn to a4).

Modern players no longer have such options. In order to be successful in such endings, they need to keep their endgame theory fresh in mind. But even this may be not enough sometimes, because the stress of permanent time-trouble after more than 60 moves may affect your memory.

After refreshing my knowledge on this endgame I easily won it after the resumption.

101.♚a6 ♚c8 102.a4 ♚c7

106...♗f2+ then 107.♚c6, followed by the pawn's unhindered advance) 107.♖f5!, preventing the check along the g1-a7 diagonal and expelling the enemy king from the critical area.

In this game I took advantage of the adjournment at my leisure, but sometimes things could get trickier, as in the following example.

Igor Novikov
Judit Polgar
Pamplona 1991

position after 80...♚h5

As in the previous game, I had studied the theory of this endgame, but remembered only some of it. The defensive system that I adopted is the safest, but there were still some subtleties on the way to a draw.

84...♚h7?!

From a practical point of view, another inaccurate decision. It was only one year later that Pal Benko showed me a drawn position analysed by the Hungarian master Jozsef Szen (1805-1857): 84...♖a5 85.♗e6 ♖b5 86.♗f5 ♖b6 87.♚e5 ♚h5 88.♗e6 ♖b5+ 89.♚f6 ♖b4, with a draw. Benko added that it is better not to get that close to the precipice, but if it happens it is at least good to know this position.

85.♗g6+ ♔h8 86.♗f5 ♖a5 87.♖g6

87...♖b5?

Finally the losing move, but without entering in more detail, this is almost impossible for humans to grasp.

88.♔g5 ♖b2 89.♔f6 ♖h2 90.♖g3 ♖f2 91.♖h3+

The end, because after 91...♔g8 White has 92.♖a3, and mate. 1-0.

This lesson was extremely painful, since it ruined my chances of a grandmaster norm, which I had come very close to achieving. During my further career I started studying such crucial practical endgames more thoroughly, something that occasionally paid off even long after the adjournment system had been abolished. Take, for instance, the following game:

Liviu-Dieter Nisipeanu
Judit Polgar
Khanty-Mansiysk 2009

position after 84...♖b5

This was the sixth rapid game of the playoff, and I needed a draw to qualify for the next round. The position is almost identical to the previous one. I had one minute left, but this time I played confidently, as I understood the ins and outs of this endgame.

85.♔e4! ♔h6! 86.♗f7 ♖g5 87.♖h1+ ♔g7 88.♗e6 ♔f6 89.♗d7 ♔e7 90.♖h7+ ♔d6 The king has escaped from the edge of the board and enjoyed its new-found freedom until move 138, when the game was drawn. I felt so confident that I even forgot to claim a draw after 50 moves (we actually played 78 moves with this material on the board!).

Conclusions

– Young players should not underestimate the importance of old games. Many of them featured almost perfect play after the adjournment.

– Try to permanently enrich your endgame knowledge and keep the most important positions fresh in your mind. ∎

MAXIMize your Tactics

with Maxim Notkin

Find the best move in the positions below

Solutions on page 105

1. Black to move

2. Black to move

3. White to move

4. Black to move

5. White to move

6. Black to move

7. Black to move

8. Black to move

9. Black to move

Be Prepared

The eternal question remains: how do I get myself in good shape before a tournament? **MATTHEW SADLER** reviews books and DVDs that may help you to be in the right disposition.

December was an important chess month for me: I was playing my first big tournament of the year, taking part in the British Knockout Championship held parallel to the fantastic London Classic. My enthusiasm for playing is somewhat variable, but I always find preparing myself for a big tournament to be a fascinating experience. By this I don't mean opening preparation – which, to be frank, is a necessary evil and, rather depressingly, rarely feels like it helps to improve your chess – but rather the process of ensuring that all the components of your game – mental and technical – are functioning smoothly by the time the tournament starts.

One of the strange things about competition is how much of your life is dedicated to repetition. With experience, you gain understanding of the parameters you require to play optimal chess: the mood you want to be in, the skills you want to have activated before the tournament (tactics, knowledge of typical endgames, ability to reason). In time, every player develops a preparation routine for tournaments that he works through, just as he has for the tournament before that, and the tournament before that... And yet, frustratingly, getting yourself into form isn't as simple as just working through a set of

standard exercises. As a professional, I started keeping notes of the important thoughts I'd had while preparing for tournaments, hoping that the next time I could just quickly read my notes and skip all that laborious thinking. It failed miserably of course: there's a living, breathing part to being in form that you only get by actively taking part in a process of preparation. Reading passively about past experiences doesn't spark any life at all in you.

So... the puzzle of preparation is as follows: you need to follow a process to ensure that the pieces of your game that you need to play well, fall into place at exactly the right time. You want the result to be repeatable, but... the process can't be routine: it must fire your imagination and bring your thoughts to life. Designing that process for each tournament is the interesting bit! Nowadays, time for chess being rather limited, I try to combine business with pleasure by preparing for tournaments by reading books (and thus writing this column at the same time ☺). So what did my preparation for this tournament look like? Well, read on!

The most fundamental requirement to playing a good tournament is to spot simple tactics. Continually missing easy tricks is terribly bad for your morale. The higher level you play, the more you need to concentrate on the difficult

things – drawing up a plan, keeping up the purpose and drive in your play throughout a whole game. You need to assume that your sense of danger will pick up on the simple stuff; if you can't, you'll waste masses of time frantically checking and rechecking everything. Solving tactical puzzles is the obvious way, but it's hard to find the right material. Ideally you would challenge yourself with spectacular positions (which keep you interested) at a moderate level of difficulty (you want to give yourself a morale boost before and during the tournament, not destroy yourself!).

This time, I was extremely lucky to be able to turn to *One Pawn Saves the Day* and *One Knight Saves the Day* by Sergei Tkachenko, published by the new Elk and Ruby publishing house. These small-format books each contain 100 studies in which the hero is the piece in the title. The idea is very nice: in each of the studies, a pawn or knight will deliver the coup de grace in the final position. The author is a member of the very strong Ukrainian team which has scored consistently high placings in the World Chess Composition Tournaments (winning in 1997). Solving studies as training before a tournament was a recommendation of Mark Dvoretsky's, but one that always filled me with trepidation. Everyone knows the feeling of staring at a fiendish study for 15 minutes and not finding any idea at all. Not the feeling I want before a tournament! These books are excellent in three ways. Firstly, the chosen studies are exceptionally beautiful. I was constantly oohing and aahing with satisfaction! Secondly, the examples are a good mix of the famous and the unfamiliar. I've solved a fair number of studies in the past, but about 75% of the studies in each book were unfamiliar to me, which is excellent. Thirdly, the level of the studies is very rewarding. Some are harder than others, but the knowledge that a pawn (in the first book) or a knight (in the second book) will deliver the final blow is a wonderful hint that always helps you in the right direction without revealing too much. I worked through all 200 before and during the tournament and I felt that it had helped immensely. Can't wait until the next pieces! My favourite of the two books was *One Knight Saves the Day*. I'll just spoil one position for you to give you an idea of the beauty of these positions (turn away now if you want to be able to solve all 100!)

One Pawn Saves the Day
by Sergei Tkachenko
Elk and Ruby, 2017
★★★★☆

One Knight Saves the Day
by Sergei Tkachenko
Elk and Ruby, 2017
★★★★☆

Gurvich 1927

1.♗c6+ ♖xc6 2.♘d7+ ♔b7
3.♖b8+ ♔xa6 4.♖b6+ ♖xb6
5.♘c5# Aaaah! So neat! Definitely recommended!

■ ■ ■

The next book on my list was Russell Enterprises' reissue of Wilhelm Steinitz's classic *The Modern Chess Instructor*. I've been an avid reader of chess books from my youth, but I can't remember having read this classic work before. I'm always keen before a tournament to review the basics of chess once more as I feel it helps me play normal positions better. I thought that the founding father of positional play would be the ideal man for the job! This book combines both Part I (published in 1889), which contains an introduction to the rules of chess, an explanation of technical terms, some thoughts on modern play and general precepts, some analysis of a series of King's Pawn Openings (the bulk of the book) and annotations to

the Steinitz-Chigorin match of 1889, and Part II (published in 1895), which adds some analysis of the Ponziani opening and the Giuoco Piano.

Ah my goodness, I was so disappointed! My disappointment may have been exaggerated because I was reading it for a specific purpose; I'm sure I would have been milder if I was just reading it as a historical work. Reading it now while looking to relearn existing knowledge, I found it

can be given up by either party at any stage of the game without at least greatly endangering the result, unless it can soon be recovered' with the assertion later on that 'For instance, the Bishop's Gambit and the Salvio Gambit show that though the king has to move early, and is deprived of the right of castling, a strong attack can be formed with the minor pieces, owing to the queen being brought out early into the adverse game'.

'Frustratingly, getting yourself into form isn't as simple as just working through a set of standard exercises.'

a very bizarre work. 'Who was Steinitz writing for?', was my first thought. The opening five chapters are aimed at complete novices of the game (the rules of the game are explained as well as the etiquette of the game, and some advice on how to train). However, Chapter VI lurches on to a short essay about 'The Modern School and its Tendency', a considerable portion of which is devoted to a description of how 'the king, though apparently on the defensive for some time, is brought into the action early in the game, and after withstanding a seemingly vehement attack, obtains perfect security with the superior position generally for the ending'. In the context of the first five chapters, I shudder to think of the effect of these words on a beginner! It's also strange to read the sober opening paragraphs, in which it is stated that 'among first-class players of equal strength, not a single pawn

The next chapter on the 'Relative Value of Pieces and Principles of Play' is also peculiar in the sense that much of the advice given on the bishop and the knight is only applicable to games that have started 1.e4 e5. Good general advice is interspersed with strange advice such as 'it is very rarely of advantage to pin an adverse knight'.

The sections on opening systems are inevitably dated, but what is strange is that you cannot relate most of the lines presented to any of the principles Steinitz explains, indeed he makes little attempt to link the two. All in all, I learnt less than I had hoped, and was unexpectedly irritated by much of it! The one thing I did enjoy was playing through the games of the Chigorin-Steinitz match. You know, 130 years ago, the chess world had already seen a match between Alpha Zero and Stockfish. Look at

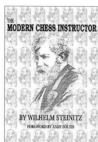

**The Modern Chess
Instructor by
Wilhelm Steinitz
Russell Enterprises,
2017**
★★☆☆☆

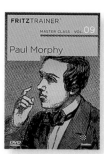

**Master Class Vol. 9:
Paul Morphy
FritzTrainer DVD
by Müller / Marin /
Reeh / Lampert
ChessBase, 2017**
★★★★☆

this game, played in consultation after the main match had ended, and you'll see what I mean:

**Chigorin/Ponce
Steinitz/Gavilan**
Havana 1889 (1)
Evans Gambit

**1.e4 e5 2.♘f3 ♘c6 3.♗c4 ♗c5
4.b4 ♗xb4 5.c3 ♗a5 6.0-0 ♕f6
7.d4 ♘ge7 8.d5 ♘d8 9.♕a4
♗b6 10.♗g5 ♕d6 11.♘a3 c6
12.♖ad1 ♕b8**

**13.♗xe7 ♔xe7 14.d6+ ♔f8
15.♕b4 f6 16.♗b3 ♘f7 17.♘h4
g6 18.♔h1 ♗d8 19.f4 exf4
20.♗xf7 ♔xf7 21.e5 fxe5
22.♖xf4+**

**22...♔g7 23.♘f5+ gxf5 24.♖xf5
♖g8 25.♖df1 b5 26.♕g4+** 1-0.

And just one diagram from the Alpha Zero match as a comparison.

AlphaZero-Stockfish 8
match 2017 (6)
position after 23.♗e7

In Steinitz' play, just as in Stockfish' play under these conditions, you sense the same disregard for the activity of his pieces – and the queen in particular – trusting in his/its ability to hold the position until the white attack has blown over. And Chigorin does a very good impression of Alpha Zero!

■ ■ ■

Since that hadn't worked out very well, I turned to the Chessbase DVD *Master Class Vol. 9: Paul Morphy* for some inspiration from the olden days of chess. I'm very fond of this series. Each DVD treats a different classic player and contains lectures from IMs or GMs on this player's treatment of the opening and middlegame as well as a series of puzzles taken from this player's attacks and endgames. Oliver Reeh and Karsten Müller are the core team for tactics and endgames and always do an excellent job (this DVD is no different). I confess though that my decision to buy the DVD depends on whether Mihail Marin is doing the middlegame section. I was intrigued to learn what Marin would discover in Morphy's middlegame play. Many moons ago, I remember GM Chris Ward – while writing a book on Morphy – bemoaning the difficulty of drawing lessons from Morphy's play due to

the large number of odds games and the dubious level of many of his opponents. Once again however, Marin comes up trumps. He picks out five games of Morphy, none of which were familiar to me, and his treatment of four of these – two games from his 1858 match against Harrwitz, a consultation game against Staunton and the last game of his 1858 match against Adolf Anderssen – is stunning. I particularly enjoyed his examination of the two blocked Dutch defences against Harrwitz:

Daniel Harrwitz-Paul Morphy
Paris 1858 (3rd match game)
position after 13...♕g6

Daniel Harrwitz-Paul Morphy
Paris 1858 (7th match game)
position after 11.f4

Marin's analysis of these games works on several levels. Firstly, I found his thoughts on these types of blocked positions to be interesting in themselves. Secondly, he does an excellent

'I ended the series of lectures with a heightened respect for both Morphy and Marin!'

job of conveying the logic and purpose of Morphy's play (especially striking in such difficult strategical positions) even when pointing out mistakes or inaccuracies in his play. I ended the series of lectures with a heightened respect for both Morphy and Marin!

■ ■ ■

While hunting around the ChessBase shop, I also ran into another couple of DVD's that caught my fancy. Ideally, preparing for a tournament would also improve your chess skills in some way. That's why I resent preparing openings for tournaments, because most of that time is spent revising your lines and trying to remember what you wanted to play, which never feels particularly useful in the long term (I'll forget them again within a few weeks anyway!). Watching a DVD like *Power Strategy 1* by Mihail Marin does give you the feeling of improving as you watch. The goal of this series is to examine general rules in chess. In this DVD, Marin takes the concept of development in the opening and the transition to the middlegame and examines a whole range of issues associated with this. For example, a player deviates from natural development and is punished for it, developing sacrifices (in which Tal features heavily as you would

expect!) and the tactical benefits of being well-developed.

At the risk of sounding like a Marin groupie, this is such a good DVD! The very first game captures your imagination and sets the scene beautifully for the rest of the DVD. It's a game Ivkov-Gheorghiu, Buenos Aires 1979. Marin describes that he first saw this game when he was 14 and it made a huge impression on him. Both his favourite opening variation and a hero of Romanian chess were defeated in very impressive fashion. The game started promisingly as Gheorghiu came up with a stunning idea for counterplay in a typical Romanian variation:

Borislav Ivkov
Florin Gheorghiu
Buenos Aires 1979
King's Indian, Larsen Variation

1.d4 ♘f6 2.c4 c5 3.d5 g6 4.♘c3 ♗g7 5.e4 d6 6.♘f3 0-0 7.h3 e6 8.♗d3 exd5 9.exd5 ♖e8+ 10.♗e3 b5

Marin dissects beautifully why such an idea might work and why it might fail, taking a tour around the white and black positions discussing the strengths and weaknesses of both. He

also draws some interesting general conclusions. For example, after 11.♘xb5, Black followed up with 11...♘e4.

Marin notes that Black is trying to justify a sacrifice by moving an already developed piece while his queenside is still undeveloped and says that you should start to have some doubts. If some of Black's active pieces are exchanged, he will be left just with his undeveloped queenside pieces. Of White's good reaction 12.0-0, Marin states that 'when you are better-developed, there is one good way to keep this advantage: keep on developing!' His explanation after 11.♘xb5 ♘e4 12.0-0 ♗xb2 13.♗xe4 ♖xe4 14.♕c2 ♖xe3 15.♕xb2 ♖xf3 of White's stunning reaction 16.♖fe1 is also very instructive:

'The line looked so beautiful for Black, so creative. But just one developing move – 16.♖fe1 – and Black is dead.'
16...♗d7 17.gxf3 ♕g5+ 18.♔h1 ♘a6 19.♘xd6 ♗xh3 and now, as Marin points out, 20.♕h8+ would have won on the spot!

I liked very much how Marin later brought in a game by Tal against Vladimirov that contains echoes of this one:

Evgeny Vladimirov-Mikhail Tal
Tallinn rapid 1988
position after 16.♕xh6

Same structure... different result though. But well... Black is Tal. Here he made the developing move **16...♗xh3!** and Black won a brilliant attacking game.

In conclusion, definitely the best examination out there of the problems and challenges of development in the early stages of the game. 100% recommended!

■ ■ ■

Another one of my favourite ChessBase authors – Sergei Tiviakov – also brought out a new DVD entitled *Realizing an Advantage*, a continuation of his series on strategy which until now has covered *The Art of Defence* and *The Art of the Positional Exchange Sacrifice*. The core of the DVD is comprised of 20 videos, divided up into different techniques of realising an advantage such as 'converting one type of advantage into another' and 'how to exploit 2 weaknesses'. One of the features of Tiviakov's instructional DVD's that most appeals to me is the standard format he uses: he introduces each theme with a classical game – he makes heavy use of the games of his heroes Karpov, Smyslov and Petrosian – and then presents some of his own games where he applied the technique he has

Realizing an Advantage FritzTrainer DVD by Sergei Tiviakov ChessBase, 2017
★★★★☆

just described. I find this approach works very well for me. I find classic games much easier to remember than modern games (possibly due to the aura of the names involved, possibly because classic games are normally slightly simpler than modern games), so these become my blueprints for practical play. However, I also find the examples of classic themes being applied in modern games very motivational: if they can do it, so can I! Tiviakov's delivery in English is sometimes rather stilted, but he compensates for this by the excellent organisation of his material and the clarity of his examples. I felt I learned a lot!

■ ■ ■

The last book in this review contains no chess whatsoever! *Maxime Vachier-Lagrave Joueur d' Echecs* by Maxime Vachier-Lagrave and Chris-

Maxime Vachier-Lagrave Joueur d' Echecs by Maxime Vachier-Lagrave / Christophe Quillien Fayard, 2017
★★★☆☆

tophe Quillien, published by Fayard, is a French-language account of what it is like to be a top professional chess player in the modern age. There are no diagrams and no chess moves in this book. The book is made up of 39 fairly short chapters, each of which is a reflection on a particular theme of MVL's life as a professional chess player, such as his coach, the job of a trainer, women in chess, life during a chess tournament, alcohol and work

outside a chess tournament. It's both a rather dull book and a very interesting one! It's dull in the sense that the tone of the book is quite down-to-earth and matter-of-fact. I remember my professional career as an emotional roller-coaster in which stress and uncertainty were my constant companions, and marked by many moments of bitter self-recrimination after defeat. I remember several moments of walking through the streets of some foreign city in tears, feeling like the world had collapsed after a time-trouble error, or one of those dreadful games where you never get started and lose with a feeling of total powerlessness. MVL reflects on a few bad moments in his career but the overall impression is somewhat flat. However, the interest of the book lies in the fact that a top player discusses elements of his life and profession that are rarely talked

> **'The interest of the book lies in the fact that a top player discusses elements of his life and profession that are rarely talked about in a relaxed and open manner.'**

about in a relaxed and open manner. What do you spend your time on when you aren't playing chess? Are you lazy? Can you concentrate well? All the questions that a non-chess player might fire at a chess player are dealt with here. I read it quickly and with pleasure, which can't be a bad sign! I'd rate it somewhere between 3 and 4 stars... Well MVL has so many Elo points, he can make do with 1 star less! 3 stars! ■

A new approach in chess improvement for youngsters

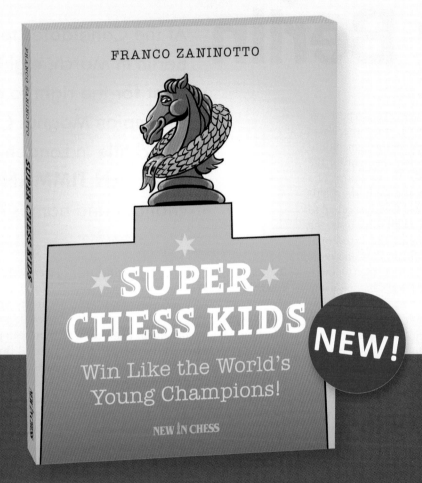

Kids who want to improve in chess often find instructional material based on games played long ago by old masters with who they have no affinity at all. Franco Zaninotto has a different approach. He knows from experience how stimulating it is to study the games of the best players in your peer group.

Zaninotto teaches elementary strategy and tactics by using games he has selected from recent Junior Championships all over the world. You will learn how to evaluate your position, recognize weaknesses in your opponent's position, develop a plan, and calculate moves of attack and defence. You will also see typical errors that even the best young players tend to make. Included are more than 100 strategic and tactical exercises. There is little excuse for not finding the winning moves: after all, other kids already did!

paperback | 144 pages | €14.95 | available at your local (chess)bookseller or at newinchess.com | a NEW IN CHESS publication

Jan Timman

Place your bets for Berlin

At the Candidates tournament in Berlin in March, eight players will fight for the right to challenge World Champion Magnus Carlsen for the world title in London eight months later. **JAN TIMMAN** looks at their chances and names his favourite.

For many years in post-war chess history, there was an established schedule to regulate the fight for the highest chess title. In the course of a three-year cycle, the would-be Challenger of the World Champion had to battle his way through three tests: the Zonal Tournament, the Interzonal Tournament and finally the Candidates Tournament. These were then followed by the 24-game World Championship match, twice as many games as these days. This schedule remained in force for five cycles, with only the format of the Candidates tournament subjected to change. Initially, in Budapest 1950, it took the form of a two-round tournament with 12 participants; later, in Bled-Zagreb-Belgrade 1959 and Curaçao 1962, it was a marathon tournament with eight players meeting one another four times: 28 games in total, also precisely twice the number of games in the present Candidates.

After the 1962 Curaçao tournament Fischer accused the Soviets of banding together against the rest, which led to FIDE replacing the Candidates tournament by matches. For a long time, no Candidates tournaments were held until, in 1985, a 16-player tournament in Montpellier was billed as such. However, the Montpellier event was followed by Candidates matches, meaning that 'Candidates tournament' was a misnomer, since the winner was not granted the status of challenger. So it's fair to say that the Candidates was only reinstated in its old glory half a century later, because in 2013, the 'new-style' Candidates Tournament was held in London.

Bull's eye

The Candidates tournament planned for Berlin this March will be the fourth one in this series and again attracts quite a wide interest. Almost everyone is interested to know who the new Challenger will be. In this regard, FIDE has scored a bull's eye. The qualification system leading up to the tournament, however, leaves much to be desired. First of all, the wildcard. This is obviously an attractive addition for the sponsor, but it also introduces an impurity in the system. Chess ought to be strong enough publicity-wise to obviate the need for such measures.

The two rating-based qualification places are justified – the Elo system is functioning well – but the names of the two players concerned should be made public earlier on; otherwise a number of players will not know what to aim for in the World Cup and the later stages of the Grand Prix. It would also be better to return to the format of one or two Interzonal tournaments, because the present system contains impurities. The World Cup organ-izers were understandably happy with World Champion Magnus Carlsen's surprising decision to take part, but it could have led to anomalous situations. Suppose that a 2750+ player had passed through the first five rounds with flying colours, only to tie 1-1 with Carlsen in the semi-final. If he were then to lose the ensuing tie-break, he would automatically be eliminated. I don't need to spell out to you how unjust that would have been.

The Grand Prix tournaments were also marred by impurities, especially because the participants only played in three of the four events. Grischuk, for example, who had not been included in the final tournament in Palma de Mallorca, had to play Giri as Black in the final round in Geneva, at which point he didn't have the foggiest idea of which result would serve him best. That depended entirely on how Radjabov and Vachier-Lagrave would fare in Palma. And these two were the only players whose qualification was at stake in that final Grand Prix tournament – a strange and unsatisfactory situation. Radjabov and Vachier-Lagrave hung in there till the final round, with the French champion suffering the worst luck of all of them. He just fell short rating-wise, got eliminated by eventual winner Aronian in the tiebreaks of the World Cup semi-finals, and didn't get the wildcard, because that was given to Kramnik. His time will surely come.

Unique achievement

But it's a good thing that Kramnik is back, because he must be regarded as a strong contender. I don't think his playing strength has diminished significantly since his defeat of Kasparov 18 years ago. The only difference is that he suffers from weak moments more often, which may be due to age. But Kramnik isn't really old. At 42, Karpov swept the board in the top tournament of Linares in 1994, finishing 2½ points ahead of Kasparov and Shirov. Another example: when Anand was two years older than Kramnik is now, he won the Candidates tournament. Kasparov, his predecessor, stopped playing at the age of 41, but fortunately Kramnik has not followed in his footsteps, although he did say a few times that he would like to bring his career to a close at some point. If he were to win in Berlin, it would be a unique achievement: a former World Champion who becomes the Challenger again 18 years after winning his title. And in a match against Carlsen, he would not be the underdog.

The same thing goes for Aronian, who is my personal favourite. Aronian has an extremely fine sense for taking the initiative, so much so that you often wonder exactly how he did it. He can be sloppy in his finishing, but not when he is in top form. So far, Aronian has never managed to find that form in a Candidates tournament, but not, I think, because he is beset by a fear of failure. I see it more as a kind of tensing-up that prevents him from playing his normal style. My own experience has taught me that this handicap reduces in severity as one gets older. Aronian is in his mid-thirties. He can still

If he manages to control his nerves, Levon Aronian should be one of the top-favourites in the Candidates tournament in Berlin.

grow stronger, especially because he was a slow developer amongst the top players. Playing in Berlin, the city where he lived for a long time, may also work to his advantage.

No outsiders

Caruana is another favourite, of course. He is a very systematic player. A consummate professional, he always tries to be as well prepared as possible. It was no coincidence that he took the lead in the recent London

same thing the last time, so I may be wrong. He did manage to put up a real challenge to Carlsen in their World Championship match in New York, after all. Karjakin can certainly not be written off. He has extensive theoretical knowledge, and is notoriously tenacious in bad positions. But I have noticed that he is more likely to lose his way when lured into unknown territory than other top players.

When it comes to it, there will be no outsiders in the Berlin tourna-

'Aronian can still grow stronger, especially because he was a slow developer.'

Classic by twice besting his opponent theoretically. Two years ago, he came within grasping distance of becoming the Challenger, but in the final two rounds he let his chances slip through his fingers. I do not doubt that he will try to make up for his failure this time. Just imagine that he succeeds in finding the same form as in St. Louis 2014, where he won his first seven games! He, too, would surely be able to hold his own against Carlsen.

Karjakin I don't think will be amongst the favourites, but I said the

ment. In principle, everyone will be in with a chance. Grischuk, the third Russian participant, is a year younger than Aronian, but has vast experience as a top player. Grischuk is a strategist first and foremost. He has a fine sense for the requirements of the position, but he usually needs a lot of time to fathom the tactical possibilities, with the result that he often ends up in raging time-trouble. This obviously doesn't help, and the problem is that time-trouble is an addiction that is hard to get rid of.

The other three players are newcomers. To introduce them, I will present you with fragments from recent games from all three of them. Mamedyarov is five years older than Karjakin, but has not moved in the highest echelons for as long. In the Nutcrackers Battle of the Generations held in Moscow in December, he scored very well, propelling himself to third place in the world rankings. A fragment from that tournament:

Andrey Esipenko
Shakhriyar Mamedyarov
Moscow 2017

position after 15.h3

A position that has arisen out of the Slav. The 15-year-old White player has withdrawn his king's bishop from c4 and fianchettoed it. This is an interesting plan, which offers chances

of an advantage. Mamedyarov now plays a sharp move.
15...c5 This advance is based on sharp calculation.
16.dxe5 ♘xe5

17.♘h4 Critical was 17.♘xe5 ♗xe5 18.♘e2, after which White is threatening to win a piece. With 18...c4! Black is able to generate just about enough counterplay. The main line goes as follows: 19.f4 ♗d6 20.e5 ♗c5+ 21.♔h2 ♗b7 22.♘c3 ♘d7 23.♘e4, and now 23...♖ad8! is the move with which Black maintains a dynamic balance.
The text is less effective.
17...g5!
Vintage Mamedyarov. He is going for the most active continuation, indicating that he is playing to win.
With 17...c4 he could have forced a draw. White has nothing better than

18.f4, after which 18...♗c5+ 19.♔h2 ♘eg4+ 20.hxg4 ♘xg4+ 21.♔h1 ♘f2+ leads to a draw by perpetual check.
18.♘f5 ♗xf5 19.exf5 ♖ad8 20.a4 b4 21.♘d5 ♘xd5 22.♖xd5 ♘d7
The alternative was 22...c4, intending to take the knight to d3, but the text is a sound practical choice, because it presents White with a difficult choice.

23.f6 A strategic pawn sacrifice that completely fails to do its job. He should have gone 23.♗e3, when it looks as if he will be in trouble because Black can take on g3 at some point. But this is not so terrible. Black has two knight moves:
A) 23...♘b6 24.♖dd1 ♗xg3 25.a5! ♘d7 26.♕c4, and White is slightly better because the black a-pawn is very weak;
B) 23...♘f6 24.♖dd1 ♗xg3 25.♕xc5, and the position is equal.

23...♘xf6 24.♖f5 ♖e1+ 25.♔h2

25...♘h5! Now it's not White but Black that gets an attack.
26.♕b3 ♘g7 Good enough, but the computer regards 26...♖e2 27.♔g1 ♗xg3! as stronger.
27.♖f6 c4 28.♕f3 h5

Winning. White will be unable to prevent the continued advance of the h-pawn. Mamedyarov provides us with an attractive finale.
29.♖h6 h4 30.♕g4 hxg3+ 31.fxg3 ♕c5 32.h4 ♗xg3+ 33.♕xg3 ♕g1+ 34.♔h3 ♖d3 35.♗f3 ♖xf3 36.♕xf3 g4+ 37.♕xg4 ♕h1+ 38.♔g3 ♖g1+ White resigned.

This fragment is a good illustration of Mamedyarov's aggressive style. He is an attractive player who is not afraid of taking risks. He seems to relish break-neck complications and usually manages to find his way through. In the past, Mamedyarov tended to be easily discouraged, often resigning too quickly, but this seems to have changed of late – and he does not lose very often. If he remains mentally strong, Mamedyarov has a good chance to finish high in the standings.

Strong technique

Wesley So just missed qualification in the previous cycle. Subsequent to this, he was untouchable in the sense that he had a long unbeaten run of 67 games of classical chess at top level. In the past year, his play suffered a slight decline. He is at his best in simple positions.

Vishy Anand
Wesley So
London 2017 (9)

position after 23...♕xd8

Nothing much seems to be going on, but Black is still a tad better; his knight pair is more versatile.
24.♕d3 A tacit draw offer. But Black is not forced to swap the queens. 24.♘f3 would have been slightly more accurate.
24...♕e7 25.♘c2 ♘f4 26.♕d2 ♘6d5
So has positioned his knights for battle. White must be wary now.
27.♔f1
He doesn't see the danger. In the endgame, you tend to prefer to keep your king away from the edge of the board, but for tactical reasons 27.♔h2 would have been better here.

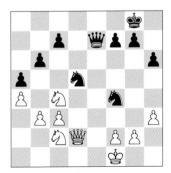

27...♘xc3! A strong knight offer that White cannot afford to accept. After 28.♕xc3 ♕e2+ 29.♔g1 ♕d1+ 30.♔h2 ♘e2 he would be mated.
28.♘4e3
Anand definitely didn't have his day. With the tactical counter-stroke 28.♘xb6! he could have restricted the damage. The point becomes clear after 28...cxb6 29.♕xc3 ♕e2+ 30.♔g1 ♕d1+ 31.♔h2 ♘e2 32.♕c8+ ♔h7 33.♕f5+, and White has perpetual check. Stronger is 30...♕e4! (instead of 30...♕d1+) – after 31.♘e3 ♘e2+ 32.♔f1 ♘d4 Black retains good winning chances.
28...♘e4
Now Black is a pawn ahead in a better position.
29.♕d4 c5

Forcing back the queen. The technical stage was not difficult for Black.
30.♕d1 ♕f6 31.♘g4 ♕c3 32.♘ce3 h5 33.♘h2 ♕b2
White resigned.

So is first and foremost a solid player who relies on his strong technique. He is a year younger than Caruana and has every possibility to develop further. At this point, I don't think he has the punching power to secure a large plus score.

First Chinese Candidate

Ding Liren is the first Chinese GM to qualify for the Candidates. He has an original playing style and his games are dotted with interesting ideas. I need only mention his fantastic game against Bai Jinshi published in New

In Chess 2017/8. At the same time, he can also play excellent technical games.

Ding Liren
Wang Hao
Tbilisi 2017 (4.2)

position after 16...♖a7

In the main line of the Catalan, White finds it hard to get an advantage. Ding Liren refuses to be discouraged by the opposite-coloured bishops and goes for a straightforward strategic plan.
17.a5!
With the eventual aim of swapping his a-pawn for the black b-pawn.
17...♘a6 18.♕b6 ♕a8 19.♘e4 ♗d8 20.♕b2 ♘b8

21.♘d6!
Now Black is more or less forced to take on a5, for otherwise White will take his knight to c4.
21...♗xa5 22.♘xb7 ♕xb7
Wang Hao decides to go for a strategically suspect endgame: he is stuck with a backward pawn and a passive knight.
The alternative was 22...♖xb7 23.♖xa5 ♕xa5 24.♕xb7 c5, after which White also gets a superior

bishop after 25.d5 exd5 26.♗xd5 ♘a6 27.♗c4 ♘c7 28.♖d1, with a lasting advantage.
23.♕xb7 ♖xb7 24.♖xa5 ♖c8 25.♖c1 ♖bc7 26.♖a8 ♔f8 27.h4

The white pieces have taken up their optimal positions, and now Ding Liren starts increasing the pressure on the enemy position with pawn moves. The first one to advance is the h-pawn.
27...♔e7 28.h5 ♔d6 29.e4
And now the e-pawn.
29...♔e7 30.e5 ♖d8 31.♔g2 ♖b7 32.♖c4 f6 33.♗e4!
Very systematic. The way for the f-pawn is cleared.
33...fxe5
It's hard to be sure, but it seems to me that this is the decisive error. White now gets a powerful majority on the kingside. Better was 33...♖b5.
34.dxe5 ♖b2

35.♗g6!
Wang Hao must have underestimated this plan.
35...♘d7 36.♖a7 ♖e2 37.♖e4
White has no objection against a rook swap; he is allowed to keep his more active one.
37...♖xe4 38.♗xe4 ♖c8 39.f4

♔d8 40.♔f3 c5 41.♔e3 ♖c7 42.♖a8+ ♔c8 43.♖a6 ♔e7 44.♖a7 c4 45.♔d2 c3+ 46.♔c2 ♔d8 47.♗d3 ♖c5

48.♖a8+
For the second time, Ding Liren uses this manoeuvre to gain a tempo.
48...♔e7 49.♖a7 ♔d8 50.♖a3
Winning the c-pawn, after which the white kingside majority decides the issue.
50...♘b6 51.♖xc3 ♖xc3+ 52.♔xc3 ♘d5+ 53.♔d4 ♔e7 54.♗e4 ♘b4 55.♔c5 ♘a2 56.♔c4 ♘c1 57.♗d3
Black resigned.

Besides Caruana and So, Ding Liren is the third player younger than Carlsen. It will be interesting to see how he will develop from here. In Berlin, he will undoubtedly provide some surprises, although I don't foresee any serious possibility of him winning the tournament. Maybe next time.

The final score
An interesting question is how many points the winner in Berlin will garner. Tal holds the absolute record as regards scores in Candidates tournaments. In 1959, he scored 20 out of 28 (16 wins and four losses)! Its equivalent in Berlin would be 10 out of 14. In the previous three editions, the winner invariably scored a relatively modest 8½ points. No player was ever in top form in any of the three tournaments. My prediction is that it will be different this time, and that the Challenger will get to nine points. ∎

MAXIMize your Tactics Solutions

1. Balashov-Jansa
Acqui Terme 2017

38...♖e2+ 39.♔h1 ♕xf3+! White resigned as he is checkmated after 40.♖xf3 ♖e1+ 41.♔g2 ♖g1 mate.

2. Gelfand-Artemiev
Moscow 2017

43...♕xf4! Threatening 44...♕g4 mate. **44.♕b7+** 44.gxf4 ♖d3+ and mate. **44...♔h6 45.♕e4 ♕f1+!** And 46.♖xf1 ♖h2 is mate again.

3. Sipila-Kanep
Finland 2017

38.♗e5! ♖xe5 Or 38...♖xe2 39.♖h8 mate. **39.♖g5+! ♔h7 40.♕h5+ ♕h6 41.♕f7+ ♔h8 42.♖exe5 ♖f8 43.♕h5** And White won.

4. Sanal-Rublevsky
Serbia 2017

51...♖f4! 52.♗xf4 gxf4 53.♔f2 The only way to maintain material equality, but it doesn't save the game. **53...h2 54.♔g2 hxg1♕+ 55.♔xg1 b4!** The final touch. White resigned.

5. Quparadze-Chu Wei Chao
Stavanger 2017

47.♖e4+ ♔g5 48.♘h7+ ♔h4 49.g5+ ♔h5 And now **50.♖xc4!** bxc4 51.♘f6+ ♔h4 51...♔xg5 allows 52.♘e4+. **52.gxh6** Black resigned as the attempt to stop the pawn by 52...♖d8 leads to mate after 53.f4.

6. Moreno-Dvirnyy
Spain 2017

Black exploited the power of his passed pawn by giving it up: **51...♖c2+** In order to control the c8-square. **52.♔e1 d2+! 53.♖xd2 ♖c7! 54.♖f2 ♗h5** The knight is trapped. White resigned.

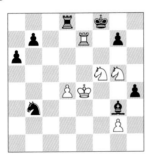

7. Ghaem Maghami-Bosiocic
Khomeyn 2017

45...♖xd4+! 46.♘xd4 If the king moves, one of the black pieces lands on f4 with crushing effect: 46.♔e3 ♗f4+ or 46.♔f3 ♖f4+. **46...♘d2+!** White resigned as after 47.♔d3 ♖xe7 48.♔xd2 ♗f4+ he is three pawns down.

8. Nenezic-Popovic
Serbia 2017

28...♖xb5! 29.cxb5 ♕c3+ 30.♔f1 ♕h3+! Not regaining the rook yet. This subtle check deprives the white king of the escape route via g2. **31.♔e1 ♕d3** And if 32.♕e4 then again 32...♕c3+. White resigned.

9. Zlatanovic-Antic
Serbia 2017

50...d3! 51.cxd3 If 51.♗xd3 ♕c5+ 52.♔h2 ♗d5 followed by 53...♖f2+. **51...♖fxe4! 52.dxe4** On 52.♖xe4 ♖a5 53.♖e7 with the idea 53...♕g3+ 54.♕g2 Black has 53...♕c5+. **52...♖a5** 'Suddenly' the queen is trapped!

David Howell

CURRENT ELO: 2682

DATE OF BIRTH: November 14, 1990

PLACE OF BIRTH: Eastbourne, United Kingdom

PLACE OF RESIDENCE: London, United Kingdom

What is your favourite city?
Singapore! But St. Louis and London are my favourite chess cities.

What was the last great meal you had?
At a membership bar in London called 'The Chess Club'. Top-class chef and some of my closest friends. They also served us ice cream on a chessboard.

What drink brings a smile to your face?
Sherry.

Which book would you give to a dear friend?
The Winter King by Bernard Cornwell. Or, if I wanted to see the look on their face, then *The Mating Game* by Jovanka Houska and James Essinger.

What book is currently on your bedside table?
There's a large pile! But among them is *New In Chess Yearbook* 125 ☺.

What is your all-time favourite movie?
Because it was Christmas recently, I'll say *Love Actually*.

Do you have a favourite actor?
I've always wanted to look like Brad Pitt.

And a favourite actress?
Neve Campbell (in *Three to Tango*).

What music are you currently listening to?
Despacito!

Who is your favourite chess player?
Karpov, for his clarity of thought.

Is there a chess book that had a profound influence on you?

The Seven Deadly Chess Sins by Jonathan Rowson.

What was your best result ever?
3rd place 2009 London Classic (behind only Carlsen and Kramnik) or winning last year's Winter Classic in St. Louis.

And the best game you played?
Howell-Sokolov, Staunton Memorial 2009, springs to mind.

What was the most exciting chess game you ever saw?
Gashimov-Grischuk, World Teams 2010.

What is your favourite square?
Maybe h8 (see Howell-Sokolov, 2009).

Do chess players have typical shortcomings?
Mine include indecision, perfectionism, and a terrible sleeping pattern.

What are chess players particularly good at (except for chess)?
Drinking and gambling.

Do you have any superstitions?
I have been known to wear light coloured socks and underwear when I play White, and darker colours as Black.

Facebook, Instagram, Snapchat, or?
None of the above. Although I still can't bring myself to delete Facebook.

How many friends do you have on Facebook?
Too many! 364.

Who do you follow on Twitter?
Chess players, minor celebrities, and my friend's cat.

What is your life motto?
'If you stumble, make it part of the dance.'

Who or what would you like to be if you weren't yourself?
Brad Pitt.

Which three people would you like to invite for dinner?
My mother, my sister, and my late father.

What is the best piece of advice you were ever given?
'You'll be a decent player someday if you play more slowly and actually think about your moves' – 20 years of time scrambles later, here I am.

Is there something you'd love to learn?
Salsa and Irish dancing.

Where is your favourite place in the world?
The west coast of Ireland is both beautiful and wild.

How do you relax?
With the help of a computer game, a good book, or a tennis racket.

If you could change one thing in the chess world, what would it be?
My own FIDE rating.

Is a knowledge of chess useful in everyday life?
Rarely!

What is the best thing that was ever said about chess?
'The passion for playing chess is one of the most unaccountable in the world...'
– H.G.Wells